T0258445

Introduction to
GANGS in
AMERICA

Introduction to
GANGS in
AMERICA

Ronald M. Holmes
Richard Tewksbury
George E. Higgins

CRC Press
Taylor & Francis Group
Boca Raton   London   New York

CRC Press is an imprint of the
Taylor & Francis Group, an **informa** business

CRC Press
Taylor & Francis Group
6000 Broken Sound Parkway NW, Suite 300
Boca Raton, FL 33487-2742

International Standard Book Number: 978-1-4398-6945-1 (Hardback)

Library of Congress Cataloging-in-Publication Data

Holmes, Ronald M.
   Introduction to gangs in America / Ronald M. Holmes, Richard
   Tewksbury, and George Higgins.
      p. cm.
   Includes bibliographical references and index.
   ISBN 978-1-4398-6945-1
   1. Gangs--United States. I. Tewksbury, Richard A. II. Higgins,
   George. III. Title.

   HV6439.U5H65 2012
   364.106'60973--dc23   2011023949

Visit the Taylor & Francis Web site at
http://www.taylorandfrancis.com

and the CRC Press Web site at
http://www.crcpress.com

To my family.
G. Higgins

*To my family, Billy Tom Holmes (2003–2010), I loved him
as a son, and to my new granddaughter, Tessa Maria.*
R. M. Holmes

Table of Contents

Preface

The topics of street gangs, prison gangs, and motorcycle gangs have always intrigued us in our teachings of criminal justice topics in the classroom. We were thinking often that the research and topics were truly inadequate to explain various items of interest to our students. Based on these concerns and issues, we decided, as many academics do, to write our own book. Little did we know how much misinformation was readily accepted as truth within the academic community and, more importantly, the true information that was available from secondary sources, such as personal interviews, books written by former bikers writing from their own experiences as "fully patched" members of a "1% motorcycle gang," a street gang of young men and women bent on a life of crime, and those in prison who had been members of outlaw groups on the streets, towns, villages of the United States as well as foreign countries.

We decided to divide the books into three sections: street gangs, prison gangs, and motorcycle clubs, especially the 1%ers. George Higgins decided that he would prefer to deal with the streets gangs. Richard Tewksbury has a special interest in prisons and prison gangs, and Ronald Holmes has a special interest in motorcycle gangs, which will become apparent when the reader arrives at that section of the book.

In writing any section of a book of this type, it is apparent that there are many people who deserve special praise and attention. To make a list of those people is truly dangerous because there is always a chance that we may forget someone, but in this case, this is a chance we will take. First of all, we thank:

- Rick Sanders (Retired, DEA; Chief of Police, Jeffersontown, Kentucky Police Department)
- Spike (Louisville Outlaw Member)
- Louisville Metropolitan Police Department
- Drug Enforcement Administration
- Federal Bureau of Investigation
- Terry Holmes, (PhD, Jefferson County, Kentucky Board of Education)

There are other agencies and others who do not fit into any particular category, but nonetheless merit special thanks. Of course, our wives and families are deserving, as always. Family members are continually concerned about what our latest interests are and what we are currently researching.

Tewksbury has a wealth of scholarly research in the area of deviant behavior and sexual alternatives. Higgins is nationally known for his work in cyber-crime, and Holmes has a special interest in serial murder and psychological profiling, and the three all have a special interest in the students in their classes.

Gangs

1

Introduction

Whenever the term "gang" is used or heard, individuals undoubtedly get a mental picture of a particular type of person, most probably someone threatening, or a minority, or someone that is easily recognizable as a "bad guy." That is to be expected because the primary types of images and messages we receive in our society fit with these stereotypes. While the messages and images about gang members that are common in our news and entertainment media are clearly based on stereotypes, there is also a large degree of truth and accuracy to many of these messages and images.

The truth is that gangs and gang members are difficult to profile. Therefore, in this first chapter, our goal is to provide a general overview of what a gang is, who are commonly found as gang members, and what types of structures and activities are common for gangs and their members. This chapter is not meant to provide information that will allow the reader to go out and easily and accurately identify gang members. That is, this chapter is not able to assist individuals or groups in determining who is or is not in a gang. Instead, this chapter is designed to help individuals understand the structure of gangs, examples of gangs and gang members, and gang members and their victimization or victimizers.

The Structure of Gangs

Gangs do not have a universal, specific structure (McGloin, 2007). Gangs and gang members come from all lifestyles: Demographics (age, sex, race/ethnicity), setting (street, prison, or motorcycle), type (social, delinquent, or violent), and purpose (defensive or turf defense) or degree of criminality (minor or serious), level of organization (simple or corporate vertical or horizontal), and function (cultural or instrumental) can and do vary quite widely across the full range of "gangs" (Spergel, 1990).

Generally, gangs have a loose structure. Many gangs may only last for a short period of time (i.e., weeks, months, or a year), but then they break up (Klein and Maxson, 1989; Curry and Decker, 1998). When gangs are operational, they often function using a traditional, hierarchical structure.

1

That is, power and influence within gangs tend to be organized vertically and tend to focus on area. Gangs also are usually fairly restricted in terms of the age of the individuals who are members or involved with a gang. Age-oriented gangs are generally focused on those individuals who are between the ages of 11 and 23. These gangs are generally composed of African-Americans, Hispanics, or Asians. Within these demographic groups, males are dominant, and females, if and when they are permitted to be members, are almost always found in subservient roles and do not ascend to leadership positions.

Horizontal gangs are those that tend to cut across neighborhoods. In addition, they are the types of gangs that are most likely to include youths of different ages. These gangs have tentacles that reach other cities, states, and even countries. Examples of these types of gangs are the Bloods, Crips, or Latin Kings.

The leadership of gangs, which many people think they understand from movies and television, is actually not as clearly delineated as often thought. Typical and stereotypical ideas of gang leadership are that it is static. In other words, common assumptions are that gang leadership relies on a single individual or a small group of individuals to lead the gang. Stereotypically, this individual or group of individuals are physically large, tough, have a criminal career, and possess enough charisma to exercise power (i.e., influence the other gang members). In reality, gang leadership is dynamic with shifts that occur over time and situations. The individual or group of individuals who are in leadership positions in gangs usually do not last in these positions for an extended period of time. The dynamic nature of gang leadership makes the gang difficult to control by handling the leaders of the gang. If a strategy is adopted to stop the gang by eliminating the leadership, another leader is likely to emerge and the gang will survive because gang leadership is really a function of the group instead of the individual. Regardless of the specific situation, a gang leader (like a good leader in general) is someone that has good communication skills, handles pressure well, and is admired by others in the gang.

No matter the changes that occur in gangs and gang activity, one of the most important distinguishing features of gangs and gang life is turf or territory. Early in gang research, turf was of great importance for multiple gangs in an area. Since the middle 1990s, the landscape of gang activity has changed for some areas. Klein (1995) argued that some cities have only one gang and that the city is their turf, whereas other cities have multiple gangs and turf has a greater meaning. For instance, when a city has multiple gangs, neighborhoods become the turf of interest. The turf (i.e., geographical location) is important for the maintenance and development of the gang. The gang maintains and replenishes itself by using the turf for recruitment of new members. Further, turf is important in that it provides the gang a place to perform its activities.

Types of Gangs

Numerous examples of gangs are available. To assist in making this a rational presentation of the types of gangs that exist, a number of criteria have to be considered. The two main forms of these criteria are gangs and gang members. These two forms are important because there are numerous gangs and individuals who participate in the gangs as members. First we describe the types of gangs and then the gang members.

Evaluating the main types of gangs may occur based on several different criteria. The criteria used in this chapter are the types of gang activities. These may be criminal/deviant or noncriminal/nondeviant. Some gangs are only formed with an interest in social interaction and having fun (Spergel, 1990). These gangs have a moderate level of criminal and drug activity (i.e., social and scavenger gangs). Over time, some of these gangs may evolve and develop criminal activities (as is the case with outlaw motorcycle gangs, which are discussed in Chapter 5). Other gangs form with the goals of members engaging in heavy drug use and sales. However, their "real" criminal activity is usually restricted to vandalism (i.e., party gangs) (Curry and Decker, 1998). Other gangs place a higher value on criminal activity (Klein, 1995). Some gangs solely focus on committing property crimes (i.e., instrumental crime); other gangs focus on more predatory forms of criminal activity (i.e., violence in the form of robbery and mugging); and serious delinquent gangs are involved in both serious and minor crimes. Some gangs are highly organized and the organization is for the purposes of protecting turf and business activities, which is often drug sales (Klein, 1995). These types of gangs may be street gangs or motorcycle gangs. In this chapter, we emphasize street gangs (motorcycle gangs are discussed in detail in Chapter 5 through Chapter 9).

Racial and Ethnic Gangs

One of the easiest and most obvious ways to categorize gangs is by the race and ethnicity of the gangs' members. Most often used is the distinction between gangs that are exclusively/predominantly African-American, Chicano/Hispanic, and Asian (Etter and Swymeler, 2008). When using this method to understand gangs, a number of different gangs may not be in the mix. That is, a small splinter of gangs may be overlooked. Further, the issue of racial and ethnic similarity is important to address. While there obviously are numerous opportunities for gangs to be multiracial or multiethnic, the fact is that, in the United States, gangs are mostly composed of members of similar races and ethnicities. Thus, we believe that few gangs are interracial and interethnic.

Chicano/Hispanic Gangs

Chicano gangs may have the most storied history of any other grouping of American gangs (Esbensen et al., 2008). To be clear, Chicano gangs have been present for more than 50 years and more than 500 different gangs are attributed to this ethnicity. Within these gangs, family and community ties are important. That is, these gangs have numerous members who have been with their particular gang for several generations. Involvement in these gangs means that the individual will assist other gang members in their time of need or despair. The youth who participate in these gangs are generally the most marginal individuals in their communities. This comes from their economic, social, cultural, and psychological position in their neighborhoods. These marginality factors create a substantial amount of stress, which the gang has the ability to help alleviate.

Identifying these gangs in public can be difficult because they do not favor wearing specific colors or clothing. When these gangs do wear specific colors, they tend to favor black, white, brown, and tan. In California, Chicano/Hispanic gangs wearing red is a signal that the gang resides in the north, while those that wear blue reside in the southern regions of the state. Additionally, when these gangs do wear specific clothes, they tend to favor Pendleton shirts (Esbensen et al., 2008).

Consistent with the family and community orientation that is common and important for Chicano gangs, membership in their gangs is not seen to be a phase or transition period in the gang member's life. Instead, the gang member seems to remain in the gang for an extended period, or even all of his life. Researchers have noted that membership in these types of gangs is often maintained well into middle age. This occurs because the gang is entrenched in the neighborhood and it is a true family activity.

Categorizing the Chicano/Hispanic gang may occur in two ways. First, Chicano/Hispanic gangs may be seen as an institutional entity. Viewing Chicano/Hispanic gangs in this way places an emphasis on the family connection. To be clear, the kinship and alliance that is formed in the gang becomes invaluable to the survival and life course of the individual. The closeness that comes from being part of the gang is paramount to the individual. This influences the gang member's life course because the gang becomes part of his family structure. This is exacerbated when a situation arises and the gang member is shown a substantial amount of the loyalty. Second, noninstitutionalized gang members, in contrast, are interested in getting out of the gang and out of the neighborhood.

Asian Gangs

In the United States, Asian gangs come from every conceivable portion of the Asian continent and Asian-controlled territories. Due to space limitations, this section highlights the most common Asian gangs, which include Vietnamese,

Chinese, and Filipino gangs. Entire volumes may be (and, in fact, have been) written about Asian gangs alone.

Individuals that immigrate to the United States will generally continue the same types of behaviors that they had performed in their home countries. Those in Asian gangs usually commit property crimes, but some have been violent and similar to those that are instrumental gangs. The vitality and survival of Asian gangs have occurred because of their resistance to penetration and their highly secretive nature. Further, Asian gangs that do victimize others tend to victimize only others from the same culture. This means that victims are often reluctant to report the criminal activity. Finally, Asian gang members do not behave in ways that attract a lot of attention from law enforcement. That is, they generally do not wear specific clothing and are often clean cut and respectful, easily blending into mainstream society.

Vietnamese Gangs

Vietnamese gangs are prevalent in many major cities across the United States. Their development in these cities has been derived from the empathy and sympathy that has come from the Vietnam War. Since the conclusion of that war in the 1970s, a number of Asians have immigrated to the United States, which changed its immigration laws and policies in order to serve as a safe place for South Vietnamese individuals following the conflict in their country. However, many of the individuals that took advantage of this policy change arrived here as unskilled, uneducated, young, and unable to speak English. These characteristics placed them at risk of becoming gang members because there were few legitimate avenues available for them to achieve "success."

Vietnamese gang members are often in their mid-to-late 20s. These gang members are often frustrated by their lack of success in achieving the American dream (i.e., success at school, community, and the acquisition of material goods). The gangs do not attract a substantial amount of attention because they (1) have no turf issues, (2) are highly secretive and have strong bonds of loyalty, (3) do not engage in public fighting, (4) do not have distinguishing tattoos, and (5) do not use hand signs to communicate or signal membership. These gangs do not have a strong central organization and often have a very fluid membership. Finally, Vietnamese gangs do not have strong ties to adult organizations.

Vietnamese gangs usually have a singular focus—money. These gangs use entrepreneurial means to acquire money, which include criminal activities, such as robbery, extortion, and auto theft. Their victimization base is other members of Vietnamese communities because these individuals lack the ability to understand or manipulate the American criminal justice system. The gang members may methodically stalk their victims to understand their patterns, and, when the time is right, they will use brute force and violence to coerce from victims the location of their valuables (i.e., cash, gold, or automobiles).

Because the Vietnamese gangs are not concerned with turf, they will often victimize others across numerous locations including in different states.

Chinese Gangs

These gangs have strong ties in China, Taiwan, and Hong Kong (Chin, 1990). The initial wave of Chinese immigrants who formed gangs had ties to organized crime. Primarily, these individuals emigrated from Hong Kong and formed the famed Tongs and Triads. Chinese gangs also benefited from changes in immigration laws and policy. After the 1965 Immigration and Naturalization Act, Chinese immigration to the United States grew exponentially. This created an entire generation of gang members that immigrated at an early age. The gangs that formed after this wave of immigration needed to protect themselves from what they perceived as bigotry that they encountered both in and outside of schools. The gangs recruited individuals who were vulnerable because of low job skills, inability to speak English, or those not doing well in school. Chinese gangs also displayed more organization and development because of their ties to organized crime. The Chinese gangs were able to support themselves by operating gambling establishments and providing protection for these establishments.

Chinese gangs seem to thrive on the use of extortion. A substantial portion of Chinese-American-owned businesses paid gang members for protection. Chinese gangs use extortion for monetary gain, a symbol of power, revenge, and intimidation of a victim.

Chinese Gangs have several characteristics (Chin, 1990):

1. Closely associated with organized crime.
2. Invest in legitimate business.
3. Many have national and international networks.
4. Are influenced by Chinese secret societies.
5. Involved in serious forms of property crimes and control large amounts of money.
6. Monetary profit is their main goal.
7. Victimize local businesses.
8. Not based on youthful fads.
9. Do not operate in deteriorated, poor neighborhoods.
10. They are embedded in the larger Triad culture of the Chinese community.
11. They have a hierarchical structure.

Chinese gangs are conflicting gangs. That is, these gangs have a substantial amount of intragang fighting. They are more dangerous to each other than threats from outside of the gang. These gangs do use a great deal of violence. Chin (1996) recently argued that these gangs have expanded their business repertoire by pursuing heroin and human trafficking.

Filipino Gangs

The structure of Filipino gangs is similar to that of Chicano/Hispanic gangs. This structure is based on using marginal individuals as gang members. These members are given a sense of community and family through the gang. Many of the members have generations of family who have been involved in the gangs.

Filipino gangs developed in two ways. First, they were not developed to assist members to survive in their neighborhoods, but to survive in prison. Second, Filipino gangs developed from immigration of young individuals during the 1970s and 1980s during political and civil unrest in the Philippines. With immigration, a number of individuals attending schools were faced with bigotry and a lack of understanding of cultural norms (as was also common for Chinese immigrants). These two issues led to numerous conflicts, and gangs were used as a defense mechanism for other members and their families.

African-American Gangs

African-American gangs began for a number of reasons. First, some argue that institutional racism is the primary impetus that spurred the development of African-Americans gangs. In the 1960s, the Black Panther party was formed to combat the perception and experience of institutional racism. In the late 1960s, a shift in the Black Panther party led to the development of two other groups: Bloods and Crips. Thus, the promulgation of two of the most notorious African-American gangs is based on responses to institutional racism. The gangs, similar to other racial/ethnic gangs, provide their members with a sense of belonging, identity, power, security, and discipline.

There is a fine distinction between the Bloods and the Crips. To date, one of the only ways to distinguish a Blood from a Crip is in the colors that they wear— Bloods wear red, and Crips wear blue. The distinction between these two gangs is important because it provides some insight into the divide between them. The divide is deep in that the gangs do not use words that begin with the first letter of each others' name. For example, Bloods do not use words that begin with "c" and Crips do not use words that begin with "b." Further, the clothes that these two gangs wear are so boisterous that they draw immediate attention to their gang identity. Obviously, other African-American gangs exist, but these two are the most notable.

Types of Gang Members

A key feature in distinguishing between gang members is to explore the connection between the individual and the gang. Some individuals may have stronger ties and longer lives in the gang whereas others may be more apt to spend a short amount of time in the gang. This may be a continuum of the gang membership involvement.

1. Regulars and hard-core: These individuals participate regularly. The survival of the gang matters to these individuals to the point where they have few other interests. Hard-core members are smaller in number, but much more committed to the gang. The gang is a lifestyle.
2. Peripheral members: These have a strong connection with the gang, but participate less than the regulars because they have other interests outside the gang. Thus, the commitment level is different than the regular or the hard-core.
3. Temporary members: Marginal commitment to the gang; join the gang later in life; short timer in the gang.
4. Situational members: The attachment is even looser than the temporary member and they join the gang when certain activities take place.
5. At risk: Pregang youth who do not belong to a gang but have shown an interest. They live in the neighborhoods where gangs exist.
6. Wannabe: Recruits who are preteen and know and admire the gang.
7. Veterans/Original Gangsters: These are individuals that are in their 20s to 30s who continue to participate in gang activities.
8. Auxiliary: Limited responsibility in the gang and a role that is usually reserved for female members of the gang (Sheldon, Tracy, and Brown, 2004).

This view of gang membership is one that suggests that an individual's placement on the continuum of membership has as much to do with the individual's identity apart from the gang as it does with any other factor.

Gang Members: Perpetrators and Victims

Little doubt exists that membership in a gang is dangerous. As stated earlier, Chinese gangs are more violent toward each other than external groups. For African-American gangs, Bloods and Crips are violent toward each other. This occurs for issues such as upholding secrets, lack of respect for other gangs, or placement for advancement. Thus, victimization is part of gang life. Researchers have shown that gang members are persistent victims of violent activity, and suffer the same sorts of trauma as that of war victims.

Conclusion

The ability to profile gangs and gang members is not exact. Without membership in a gang, the primary information that may be gleaned is that of structure and tendencies of members that transcend race and ethnicity (i.e., Chicano/Hispanic, Asian, and African-American). The number of gangs precludes uniformity in the understanding of gang structure and membership.

One uniform theme is that gang membership is dangerous. Many gang members are crime victims as well as crime perpetrators. The depth and breadth of gang victimization is under investigation, but to date we are convinced that a large number of gang members also have been victims.

Discussion Questions

1. Explain the typical structure of gangs.
2. What are the characteristics of Asian gangs?
3. Discuss the types of gang members.
4. Explain why race/ethnicity is so important in gang life.

Gangs and Homicide

2

Introduction

Gang members running through streets, alleys, and parks shooting at one another. Drive-by shootings coming seemingly out of nowhere and killing children playing in their yard. A drug market disrupted by a fight and then gunshots. The evening news leading off with a story about "yet another gang-related homicide in our city today … ." These images commonly come to mind when mentioning gangs and homicide. Popular beliefs hold that gang members are indiscriminate in their violence, often killing innocent bystanders and are so involved and invested in drug trafficking that they will stop at nothing to protect their market and turf. While these types of situations certainly do happen, they are far from the norm when looking at the complete picture of gangs and homicides.

In this chapter, we will discuss what social scientists know about gangs and their involvement in homicide. One of the most obvious is that many of the facts about gangs and homicide do not match the assumptions that people have. What people think they "know" about gangs and homicide is actually incorrect. Yes, killing is a problem, not only in the world of gangs, but in our society in general. Killing by and of gang members, however, is a crime problem that, while largely confined to major cities, does have effects in many communities, and for many people. This chapter will present an overview of the problem of gangs and homicide focusing on what we mean by the term "gang homicide," statistics and trends in killings by and of gang members, characteristics that are both common among gang homicides and that distinguish these types of killings from other forms of homicide, the largely "unique to gang homicide" form of violence of the drive-by shooting, and the relationship between gang homicide and other forms of criminal activities, especially drug trafficking.

Defining and Counting Gang Homicides

One of the most widely recognized facts about gangs in America is that gang members are involved in crime, especially violent crime. Violence by gang members is common, and it comes in a range of criminal offenses. According to the Bureau of Justice Statistics (Harrell, 2005), gang members

11

commit approximately 6 percent of all violent crime reported in the United States. The proportion of violent offenses that are committed by gang members, perhaps contrary to popular belief, actually decreased in the late 1990s and first decade of the twenty-first century. From a high point of approximately 10 percent of all violent crime being perpetrated by gang members in 1996, there has been a decline of nearly 40 percent to only about 6 percent of all violent crimes being gang-related.

Among violent criminal offenses, the one offense considered the most serious is homicide. When looking at all homicides in the nation, we see that the proportion committed by gang members is also approximately 6 percent (Harrell, 2005). Clearly, homicide being committed by gang members is an important issue, both for communities and law enforcement officials. Consider that in 2009, there were 13,636 homicides in the United States (Federal Bureau of Investigation, 2010). As 6 to 7 percent of these are committed by gang members, this means that, in 2009, 895 homicides were committed by gang members. While these are national statistics, in some communities (especially our largest cities), homicides committed by gang members account for between 1 in 5 to 1 in every 2 homicides (Lemmer, Bensinger, and Lurigio, 2008). Perhaps the simplest way to think about the issue of gangs and their relationship to homicide is to consider that the presence of gangs in a community is positively related to the rate and number of homicides that occur in that community (Tita and Cohen, 2004).

When discussing "gang homicides," it is important to keep in mind that what gets counted as a gang homicide will vary depending on how local law enforcement authorities define the term. In some jurisdictions, the police count all killings in which a gang member is in any way involved as a gang-related homicide. In other jurisdictions, though, only those instances in which "gang business" or some activity that is directly tied to gang activity results in a killing will be counted as a gang homicide. Whether a particular homicide is or is not officially defined as a gang-related offense is not the important point, because the harm is done and someone is dead. What is important is to remember that, as is the case with so many things in the study of gangs and crime in general, the statistics that are available are at least somewhat open to interpretation. Regardless of what is counted or how it is counted, however, the fact remains that gangs and gang members are involved in homicide—as both perpetrators and victims—and this is a very real and important problems in many communities.

The issue of what is counted and how it is counted points directly to one of the most frustrating aspects of gang homicide for researchers. Simply stated, it is very difficult to get and study data about gang homicide. As Maxson (1999, p. 199) explains about studying gang homicide, "Cases involving gang members are among the most difficult to research because the dynamics in these incidents are frequently chaotic, and, because of intimidation factors, information from witnesses is often only minimally available, these features, coupled with low levels of gang participation in homicide in most U.S. cities, have discouraged most researchers from investigating the gang aspects of homicide." What this means is that while we certainly know that some homicides are perpetrated by gang members, some homicides involve victims that are gang members, and that at least some homicides in most cities are in some way connected to a gang, we just do not have a lot of information about such events, nor do we have a large body of data and research findings to draw on when discussing data. With this in mind, this chapter presents what we do know about gangs and homicide. However, as you can see, our knowledge about this aspect of gangs is less developed than our understanding about other aspects of gangs, gang activities, and gang life.

One factor that sets gang homicides apart from other types of homicides is the fact that gang homicides primarily involve juveniles. When looking across all gang homicides, we see that the vast majority (80 percent) are committed by juveniles (Federal Bureau of Investigation, 2010). This pattern has been in place for at least a couple of decades, but in recent years there has been the start of a change in this pattern. In the last seven to ten years, there has been a slight increase in the annual number of gang homicides committed by adults. However, the fact remains that even with this change appearing there continues to be a relatively steady number (around 700 annually) of homicides committed by juvenile gang members (Federal Bureau of Investigation, 2010).

The number of gang-associated homicides in the United States dramatically increased starting in the 1990s. Whereas, from the mid-1970s until the late 1980s, the annual number of gang homicides ranged from 129 (1976) to 428 (1988), and accounted for fewer than 2 percent of all homicides (Fox and Zawitz, 2005), this changed dramatically in the next few years. Starting in 1990, there have been at least 800 gang-related homicides reported in the United States every year. The increase in gang homicides continues in the twenty-first century. Between 2000 and 2004, the number of gang murders across the nation increased 25 percent; this is especially notable as during this same time period the rate of serious, violent crime overall was decreasing. In addition, not only have the numbers of such offenses increased, but so have the proportion of all homicides increased. Beginning in 1991, the percentage of homicides in the United States that were gang related topped 4 percent, hitting a peak in 2002 of 6.9 percent.

Obviously, with nearly 1 in every 14 killings in the United States being gang-related, the problem of gang homicide is one that is widely recognized among law enforcement officials in the United States. Perhaps the strongest evidence of this can be seen in the fact that, largely in response to the continuing increase in such incidents, in 2004 the Federal Bureau of Investigation (FBI) named street gangs (and their violence) as its top priority. Because of the high levels of violence and danger posed by such groups, the FBI changed the way they referred to such groups from "youth gangs" to the more ominous and serious sounding designation of "criminal organizations and enterprises," the same way that they have referred to traditional organized crime groups.

Characteristics of Gang Homicides

In many ways, gang homicides are distinguishable from other forms of homicide. Killings by and of gang members often look very different than killings that arise out of an argument, a robbery, a sexual assault, or a domestic violence situation. Gang homicides have clear and evident patterns in the types of persons involved, where they occur, and how they occur. In this section, we will discuss the distinguishing characteristics of gang homicides based on who is involved, where such crimes tend to occur, and how the killing happens.

Who Is Involved

Looking at who is involved in gang homicides means looking at both those individuals who commit homicide and those who are the victims. As discussed earlier, "gang homicide" can include a killing in which a gang member is the one doing the killing, the one who is killed, or a case where both the victim and perpetrator are gang affiliated.

Gang members are individuals who have higher risk of being victims of homicides than other members of society. Gang members have significantly increased risks of being victims of homicides compared with those who are not members of gangs. Due to the types of activities in which gangs are involved, gang members are more often in settings, and around other persons, that improve their chance of being victimized or the opportunities to offend. The first characteristic, perhaps the most notable of persons involved in gang homicides, is that these are offenses in which juveniles are highly likely to be the offenders, and the victims. Compared with homicide in general, and all other specific forms of homicide, juveniles represent a much greater proportion of offenders and victims in gang homicides. Juveniles that are in a gang are much more likely to be involved in homicide than nongang-affiliated juveniles.

In a comparison of youth with serious official records of delinquency, Lattimore, Linster, and MacDonald (1997) showed that those youth with a history of being involved in a gang were much more likely to be killed than even serious delinquents who were not affiliated with a gang. However, this is not to say that all gang members are targeted for homicide, nor that all victims of gang homicides are gang members. Hutson et al. (1995) reported that 32.7 percent of gang-related homicide victims in Los Angeles between 1979 and 1994 were not affiliated with a gang in any way. Pizarro and McGloin (2006), drawing on five and a half years' worth of homicides in Newark, New Jersey, report that fewer than one in five (17.5 percent) of victims of gang homicides had a criminal record. However, gang members themselves remain the typical target of gang homicides. Simply being a member of a gang is one of the most significant risk factors for youth being a victim of homicide. The chances of being a victim of homicide increase by as much as 1,000 percent when an individual is a member of a gang (Decker and Van Winkle, 1996).

A second easily, noticeable characteristic of persons involved, as both offenders and victims, in gang homicides is race. Those who kill or are killed in gang homicides are typically African-American, and to a somewhat lesser extend, Hispanic. It is most common for the victim and offender in a gang homicide to be of the same race; gang homicides are most often intraracial events, not interracial. Overwhelmingly, the individuals involved in gang homicide are of the same race. The specific percentages of gang homicide offenders and victims of particular races vary across cities, primarily because the racial composition of cities varies. Nationally, the majority of both offenders (54.3 percent) and victims (57.5 percent) are white. However, the 41.2 percent of black offenders and 39 percent of black victims of gang homicides do show that minorities (especially African-Americans) are more than three times as prevalent among gang homicides than their prevalence in American society (12.4 percent) (United States Bureau of the Census, 2009). These statistics vary across locations, however. In some cities, the population is overwhelmingly African-American. For example, Newark, New Jersey, (where the population according to the U.S. Census Bureau (2009) is 50.3 percent African American), the number will vary significantly. In Newark, fully 87 percent of gang-related homicide victims and 90 percent of perpetrators have been shown to be African-American (Pizarro and McGloin, 2006). These numbers, however, still show significant over-representation of minorities in gang homicide.

The third demographic characteristic of gang homicide offenders and victims that shows a very strong pattern is sex. Homicides committed by gang members are almost always committed by males and against male victims (Fox and Zawitz, 2005; Klein and Maxson, 1989; Klein, Maxson, and Cunningham, 1991; Kubrin and Wadsworth, 2003; Pizarro and McGloin, 2006). In fact, when females are killed or injured in gang-perpetrated gun violence, they are usually injured unintentionally. According to Miller and Decker (2001) (and discussed in Chapter 8), women in gangs are typically involved in different types of activities and violence, and rarely the target of serious violence. As Miller and Decker (p. 115) conclude, "young women's greatest risk of gang homicide was being in the wrong place at the wrong time."

When we look beyond the simple demographics of age, race, and sex, however, we find some patterns and trends that would probably come as a surprise to many people. For instance, one of the interesting facts about gang homicides, and a point that distinguishes it from the majority of other homicides, is that perpetrators and victims in gang homicides frequently do not know one another and often have no previous affiliation, association, or relationship with one another (Maxson, Gordon, and Klein, 1985). Despite popular belief and media-perpetuated images and stories, the victims of gang homicides are typically not innocent community members that gang members kill for expressed purpose or in an attempt to rid a community of "straight" people. This is not to suggest that innocent bystanders are never victims of gang violence and killing, for they are, and such instances are truly tragedies. Mostly, gang homicides are events between gang members, typically members of rival gangs. Additionally, gang homicides are more likely than nongang homicides to involve multiple offenders (Klein and Maxson, 1989; Pizarro and McGloin, 2006).

Also contrary to popular assumptions and beliefs (perhaps because of what we see, hear, and read in both the news and entertainment media) is that in a majority of cases neither the offenders nor victims are usually under the influence of alcohol or drugs at the time of the incident. While many observers believe that gangs are all about drugs, and there may be some truth to this belief, when killings occur, it is only a minority of both offenders and victims that are intoxicated, or have any identifiable levels of alcohol or illicit drugs in their bodies. The presence of alcohol or drugs in offenders and victims in gang homicides is actually lower than what we see for all other types of homicides, and for assaults and robberies (Kubrin and Wadsworth, 2003).

Where Gang Homicides Occur

Just as with any form of homicide, and almost all types of crimes in general, gang homicides can and do occur in a wide range of places. However, despite the fact that such incidents can and do occur just about anywhere, there are some obvious patterns and trends in where gang homicides occur.

First, and fitting with most laypersons, assumptions and beliefs, is the fact that gang homicides, not surprisingly, are primarily a problem in large cities. As reported by the U.S. Bureau of Justice Statistics, between 1976 and 2005 nearly seven of every ten (69.3 percent) gang homicides occurred in a large city. Roughly one in seven (13.1 percent) gang homicides occurred in a small city, one in six (16.9 percent) occurred in a suburb, and almost none (one in every 142, or 0.7 percent) occurred in rural areas (Fox and Zawitz, 2005). Popular beliefs are that gangs are only a problem in large cities, but as we will see in later chapters, this is not the case. Not only are gangs present in locations outside of the largest American cities, but so too is the violence (including homicide) that is often associated with gangs present in medium-sized and smaller cities.

Gang homicides are most common in large cities, but gang homicides are most likely to happen in areas or neighborhoods of a city where there is a significantly lower income level and higher unemployment rates than in other areas of the city. Not only does this fit with our ideas (and fears?) about where it is most dangerous in regards to being killed, but this is logical when we remember that poverty and unemployment are two of the most important variables for predicting where gangs are found in the first place (Kyriacou et al., 1999). When gangs are more likely to be present, so too are the gang-related crimes likely to be present.

In addition to the fact that gang homicides are primarily an urban problem, and then even more likely a problem in poor and disadvantaged/disorganized areas of cities, there are two other aspects of where gang homicides typically occur that distinguish them from other types of homicides. First, gang homicides are more likely than nongang homicides to be committed outside, in public locations (Klein and Maxson, 1989; Pizarro and McGloin, 2006). This is likely due to there being greater opportunities for gang members to encounter one another in outdoor areas as opposed to inside of homes, businesses, schools, etc. Second, when we think of other types of homicides—domestic violence killings, robberies (especially of businesses), and arguments between family members, friends, and acquaintances—these types of situations are more likely to happen inside of buildings. So, the fact that gang homicides are most likely to occur outdoors, and in public places, is logical, and when we think about the dynamics of both gangs and homicide in general, it should be expected.

A second distinguishable characteristic of where gang homicides typically occur is that they occur farther away from the homes of both offenders and victims. Gang homicides are distinguishable, typically, from all other types of homicides in that both victims and perpetrators in gang-related homicide travel the farthest from their homes to the place where the homicide occurs (Pizarro, Corsaro, and Yu, 2007). In studying all homicides over a nine-year period (1997–2005) in Newark, New Jersey, Pizarro and her colleagues found that while domestic violence offenders and victims travelled the least distance between home and the location of the homicide (which is not surprising), gang homicides occurred the farthest away from perpetrator and victims' homes. Gang homicides are farther from the homes of those involved than is the case with drug-, argument-, or robbery-based homicides. Interestingly, it is the perpetrator in a gang-related homicide that usually travels farther to the scene of the event. In Newark, gang homicide suspects traveled an average of just over two miles to the scene of the homicide, compared to victims being an average of only

1.28 miles from home. The offenders in gang homicides also travel, on average, at least one-third farther than the offenders in all other types of homicides (Pizarro, Corsaro, and Yu, 2007).

How Gang Homicides Are Committed

Just as there are clear patterns in who is involved in gang homicides and where such offenses occur, so too are there very clear and easily identified patterns in how gang homicides are committed. The most obvious fact is that they are committed with a gun. Not only are homicides involving gang members committed with a gun, but they are typically perpetrated with a handgun. Recall that at the start of this chapter we said that whereas 6 to 7 percent of all homicides are committed by gang members, between 9 and 10 percent of all firearm homicides are committed by gang members (Harrell, 2005). This means that gang homicides are more likely than other forms of homicide to be committed by shooting the victim. The percentage of firearm homicides committed by gang members has actually been increasing in the past two decades. In the early 1990s, only about 7.5 percent of all homicides with firearms were committed by gang members, but the percent has increased to nearly 10 percent in recent years.

While handguns apparently are the preferred weapon of persons committing gang homicides, these are not the only types of guns used. A look at the types of weapons used in homicides both by and of gang members reveals that during the 1990s there was an interesting and, unfortunately, more lethal change beginning to occur in gang homicides. This increase is commonly attributed to an apparent movement of gangs toward use of semiautomatic or fully automatic firearms (Block and Block, 1993; Block and Christakos, 1995; Hutson et al., 1995). Such weapons are simply more lethal than most handguns. It was during the 1990s that the likelihood increased of a victim dying as a result of being shot in a gang assault.

There is an inextricable link between patterns and trends (e.g., increases) in gang-related homicides and trends (e.g., increases) in the frequency in which guns are used by gang members in assaults. Since 1987, more than 90 percent of all gang-perpetrated homicides are committed with a firearm. When compared with other types of homicide circumstances, such as homicides committed during the commission of another felony offense, during the course of an argument, in a domestic violence situation, or all other types of situations, gang homicides are significantly more likely to be committed using a gun (Fox and Zawitz, 2005; Kubrin and Wadsworth, 2003; Pizarro and McGloin, 2006). Generally speaking, approximately 70 to 75 percent of all homicides accompanying another felony, 60 to 65 percent of homicides arising from an argument, and 50 to 60 percent of "other" types of circumstance homicides are perpetrated with a gun (Fox and Zawitz, 2005). Clearly, gang-perpetrated homicides are incidents involving guns, and guns are far more likely to be used by gang members than other types of homicide offenders.

While guns are the apparently preferred method of gang members for committing homicide, they are certainly not the only weapon or method involved in such killings. Lopez (2006) reviewed data from official reports on homicides for the 1990s focusing on identifying the weapon/method of killing in gang-perpetrated homicides. The findings of this review of over 14,000 incidents show that handguns are clearly the preferred weapon used in over 80 percent of gang killings. However, other types of guns were used in 10.8 percent of killings, a knife was the weapon of choice in 6.1 percent of incidents, some type of blunt object (bat, pipe, etc.) was used in 1.7 percent of killings, and in 0.8 percent of incidents victims were essentially beaten to death with no weapon (Lopez, 2006). It is notable that there are some interesting trends that can be seen in weapon/method of choice by race. First, handguns are used in a larger percent of gang homicides committed by African-Americans, while other types of guns are most likely to be used by whites. Asian gang members are more likely than their white or African-American counterparts to kill via beating, either with or without some weapon (although most Asian gang killings are committed with guns) (Lopez, 2006).

Not only are there clear patterns in who is involved, where the incident occurs, and how it is committed for gang homicide, but so too is there a noticeable and distinguishing pattern in the aftermath and follow-up to gang homicides. Although the reasoning is not fully understood, there is evidence to suggest that gang homicides are more likely than other killings to result in an arrest of a perpetrator (Roberts, 2007). Analyzing homicides from 21 states in the year 2002, Roberts (2007) showed that the likelihood of a gang-perpetrated homicide resulting in clearance of the offense by law enforcement officials (e.g., arrest) may be as much as one-third higher than for other types of homicides. Alderden and Lavery (2007) studied factors related to the clearance of homicides over a 12-year period in Chicago. They focused on the factors related to the likelihood of police making an arrest in gang-related homicides as they compared to expressive homicides (in which the offender simply seeks to hurt or kill the victim) and instrumental homicides (where the offender is seeking to get some type of property or money from the victim). Five variables are important predictors of a gang-related homicide resulting in an arrest. Three characteristics of victims are important: (1) victims under the age of 26 are more likely to see a case end in an arrest, (2) white victims are more likely to see a case end in an arrest compared to cases with African-American or Hispanic victims, and (3) cases in which the victim did not have a criminal record are more likely to be solved and result in an arrest. Additionally, two characteristics of the homicide event are important in predicting an arrest in a gang-related homicide. For cases in which a weapon other than a gun was used, the likelihood of an arrest is nearly three times as high. And, homicides that occur during the daytime (between 6 a.m. and 5 p.m.) are more likely to result in a clearance of the case by arrest. Whether these differences are the result of different types of available evidence, different investigative activities by the police, or some other factors is not known, however.

In summarizing the typical situation of a gang homicide, Maxson et al. (1985, p. 215) concluded that "it is evident that gang incidents are generally more chaotic, with more people, weapons, offenses, and injuries out in the open, among people less familiar with each other." We also can add to this that gang homicides tend to be between persons of similar races, between juveniles, and to include the use of a gun. For many of us, we also can add the "good" news that gang homicides are more likely to be cleared (e.g., solved) by the police and to result in official processing (and punishment) of the offender.

Drive-By Shootings

In addition to our above discussion about how gang homicides typically occur, it is important to address the unique-to-gang-homicide method of killing in the drive-by shooting. Drive-bys as a form of homicide are known by law enforcement officials as a form of homicide that is distinctive to gangs (Hutson et al., 1994). It is exceptionally rare for homicides arising from other motivations (arguments, during the commission of some other felony, domestic violence, etc.) to occur via a drive-by shooting. The drive-by is when a vehicle with gang members inside drives to a location and shoots from the vehicle at targets they seek to kill or injure. As the name for the activity implies, the killing is done while the offender literally "drives by" the victim.

While drive-by homicides are unique to gang homicides in our culture, they are (possibly surprising for some people) really not "new" or recent developments. In fact, the urban, gang-member-perpetrated drive-by shooting is simply a slightly modified version of a not uncommon method of attack used in war and other conflicts. As Klein (1971) explains, such a method of attack was first referred to in the mid-twentieth century as "japping," based on a method of hit-and-run attacks practiced by Japanese soldiers during World War II. These methods of attack also have been referred to as "forays" (Miller, 1966), reflecting the idea of travelling and attacking simultaneously. What we see here is that gangs have simply adopted a method of attack that has been used for decades (perhaps since the early days of the automobile) for their own purposes. If we look more broadly, it may be that the drive-by shooting even precedes the introduction of the automobile. For anyone who is a fan of cowboy movies, the "ride-by" shooting can be seen in a number of westerns, where the "bad guy" (whether a cowboy, outlaw, or Indian) rides his horse by a victim, shooting as he does so. Today, instead of galloping by with a six-shooter, the drive-by is in a (frequently stolen) car containing several urban gang members.

When you think about how a drive-by shooting actually occurs, it can be seen as a smarter and safer way for an offender to carry out his violence. Drive-by shootings are practiced for purposes of attacking by surprise. Some scholars of gang activity (Hutson and Eckstein, 1996, p. 141) argue that the primary intention of gang members performing drive-by shootings is to promote fear and to intimidate rivals (the targets); actually causing harm or killing is a secondary motive for such activities. In this respect, the drive-by is seen as a way to establish status and rank for individual gang members and to make a statement of the power and abilities of the gang. A second (and practical) reason for gangs to engage in drive-by shootings is that such "is a tactic that lets gangs cope with the spread-out city and survive retaliation" (Sanders, 1994, p. 56). Here, the idea is that the rivals or targets of a particular gang's violence may be located at a significant enough distance that, to physically get to the rival's territory, it is necessary to drive rather than walk. If the gang were to walk, they would have to pass through territory where they would be noticed and, perhaps, become targets themselves. When doing a drive-by, as the shooting occurs, the shooters are already actively moving away and out of reach of their rival's possible reactions or retaliation.

Drive-by shootings by gangs are also somewhat different than many other forms and instances of violence and homicide in that they are the least likely form of gang violence to be directly associated with drug trafficking (Hutson, Anglin, and Pratt, 1994). As is discussed below, competition for market share in the local drug market is behind much, especially inter-gang, violence committed by gang members. However, drive-bys are obviously very violent events, and result in significant numbers of injuries and deaths for those who are targeted. Because of their high level of efficiency and the limitations that drive-bys put on possible retaliation, they are common forms of gang violence. Especially in large cities with significant gang presence (and violence levels), drive-by shootings may account for anywhere from one-quarter to one-half of all gang homicides (Hutson et al., 1994; 1995; Hutson and Eckstein, 1996). However, local contexts and culture also appear to be important in how common drive-by shootings are. For instance, in the early 1990s, fully one-third of gang homicides in Los Angeles were drive-by shootings, but in Chicago, drive-bys accounted for only 6 percent of gang homicides (Hutson and Eckstein, 1996; Block and Christakos, 1995).

The injuries and harms that come from drive-by shootings are not necessarily contained on intended targets. As shooting occurs from a moving vehicle, and shooters have little time to aim their shots, and coupled with the fact that drive-bys are largely intended to instill fear in rivals, it is not surprising that many of the persons hurt or killed by such actions are not shooters' intended targets. (Think about movie westerns. How often did a ride-by shooting actually result in the intended target being killed?) In Los Angeles, it is estimated that approximately one-half of the victims of drive-by shootings are children. In one year (1991), in Los Angeles a total of 677 children were shot in drive-by shootings; this computes to an average of 49 per month or more than 1.5 per day. Not only are children and adolescents frequently the victims of drive-by shootings, but so too are individuals who are not involved in gangs, drugs, or other illegal activity. At least one-third of victims of drive-by shootings are not in any way affiliated with a gang (Hutson et al., 1994). The resulting indiscriminate harm that comes from drive-by shootings also may be a function of the fact that such are the form of gang homicide in which especially young gang members are most involved (Hutson et al., 1994; 1995).

Homicide and Other Criminal Offenses

Gang homicide, like many homicides committed by and on nongang members, is often connected with other criminal activities. As we will discuss in later chapters, gangs are involved in a wide range of criminal activities. Sometimes these other crimes lead to homicide, either in the immediate or in a delayed, reactionary way. Gang homicide can be linked to general levels of crime in particular neighborhoods, to other or additional homicides and assaults, and to drug trafficking. The association of gang homicide with each of these other criminal types and conditions is discussed below.

Gang Homicide and Community Crime Rates

One important, but frequently overlooked, aspect of understanding how gangs and crime rates in the community in general are linked is to look at whether gang crime follows the emergence of overall high crime rates, or does the presence and criminal activities of gangs serve as the driving force for a community having a high rate of crime. Above we discussed how gang homicide is most likely to occur in urban communities, especially neighborhoods of cities with characteristics of social disorganization—poverty and high unemployment. Such communities are those that exhibit the highest crime rates in our society. So, the question becomes: How do the already-existing characteristics of neighborhoods and presence and violence by gangs influence one another? To answer this, we need to look at whether high rates of crime (especially violent crime, like homicide) appear in a neighborhood after gangs are established, or whether gangs emerge in communities already plagued by high rates of crime and violence. In some people's minds, this might be like a "chicken and egg" question; it is a question for which we supposedly cannot come up with an answer, and it just is not that important anyway. However, this is actually not the case.

What we see at first is that there is evidence to support either position, that gangs bring crime or that gangs become established in communities that already have high rates of violence and crime. But, while there is at least some evidence to support both positions, the majority of the research that is available primarily supports the idea that gangs develop in already crime- and violence-ridden neighborhoods (Tita, Cohen, and Engberg, 2005; Tita and Ridgeway, 2007). As such, this would mean that gangs (and the violence they bring) are largely reactions to an already disadvantaged, disorganized, and crime-ridden social environment.

The importance of understanding how the community and social factors contribute to gang homicides is clearly expressed by one researcher who explains that "[G]ang members do not kill because they are poor, Black, or young, or live in a socially disadvantaged neighborhood. Instead, they do so because they live in a structured set of social relations in which violence works its way through a series of connected individuals. ... homicides among gangs most often result from conflict over symbolic threats within group contexts that stress the use of violence as social control" (Papachristos, 2009, p. 74).

Gang Homicide and Other Homicides/Assaults

In communities where gang homicides occur, there are typically higher rates of other (e.g., nongang-related) homicides than in communities where gang homicides are not present. When gang homicides happen in communities, they frequently signal an increased likelihood of additional gun homicides, especially homicides committed by youth, coming in the near future (Cohen et al., 1998). When looking at incidents of gang-related homicides occurring in Chicago and St. Louis, researchers have shown that in the first three weeks following such an event there is a significantly decreased likelihood of a youth gun homicide, which may be the result of increased police attention in the neighborhood. However, after the three-week period, likelihood of another gang homicide returns to a high level (Cohen et al., 1998). What this tells us is that, in neighborhoods where gang homicides occur, there is a general diffusion of violence into both additional gang homicides and other types of homicides as well.

The association of gang homicides and additional future homicides being more likely in a particular neighborhood is also tied to the fact we have repeated several times, that gang homicides tend to occur in poorer and generally more socially disorganized neighborhoods (Kubrin and Wadsworth, 2003). The idea that socially disorganized neighborhoods are where gang-related homicides are most likely to occur is consistent with a long line of criminological research showing that homicides and, in fact, most types of violent crimes, are more likely in neighborhoods where economic disadvantage is concentrated and neighbors lack a strong, cohesive set of bonds among themselves.

However, when looking at gang-related homicides specifically, Kubrin and Wadsworth (2003) found that higher rates of turnover among residents are not associated with an increase in such offenses. This finding holds across different communities. Whereas Kubrin and Wadsworth (2003) established this pattern in St. Louis, Pizarro and McGloin (2006) also have shown that in Newark, New Jersey, economics is important, but high rates of resident mobility/turnover is not associated with increased rates of gang homicides. Rather, it is in neighborhoods where residents are more stable that gang homicides are more likely to occur. While at first this may appear counterintuitive, it has a relatively simple explanation. When a community is more stable and residents are more likely to stay in place for longer periods, gang members may be more entrenched in both the neighborhood and their alliances and rivalries. Therefore, animosities between gangs may be more established, and, consequently, lead to more disputes between members. As some criminologists have argued, gang homicides, especially in socially disorganized neighborhoods, are primarily about attempts by individuals to earn respect, establish a reputation for themselves, and to express frustrations with their overall living conditions (see Anderson, 1999). As a way to do this, assaulting (and possibly killing) others—especially those seen as either actually or symbolically being responsible for one's generally poor living conditions—is one of the few perceived ways to express frustration and discontent.

Many of these same ideas have been used as well to explain the generally high homicide rates in cities such as Los Angeles. When looking at the density of street gangs in neighborhoods, there is a strong correlation to levels of homicide in the community (Robinson et al., 2009). In fact, when considering not only the presence and density of gangs in a neighborhood, but also high unemployment, high rates of school dropouts, highly dense populations and concentrations of nonwhite residents (all of which are indications of high levels of social disorganization), it is possible to explain more than 90 percent of the variation in rates of homicide (Robinson et al., 2009). However, statistically the most important of these factors is the concentration of gangs. When more gangs are present within the community, homicide rates in general go up dramatically. This relationship has been shown in numerous cities across the nation (Robinson et al., 2009; Tita and Ridgeway, 2007). What this suggests is that the presence of gangs is the factor that drives the level of violence in a neighborhood and is believed to be a catalyst for both violence in general and homicide in particular.

Drug Trafficking

A third important aspect of how gang homicides are related to other forms of criminal activity is the relationship between gang homicides and drug trafficking. Said simply and directly, many gang homicides are connected to drug trafficking. Individuals (especially gang members) competing for drug customers, individuals purchasing drugs from gang members, and gang members involved in the sale and protection of drugs may all be involved as victims or offenders in gang homicides. The rapid increase in gang homicides (and perhaps all types of violence and activity) during the 1990s paralleled the emergence and rapid spread of use of crack cocaine in American cities. The crack cocaine market was initially almost completely controlled by street gangs, and, with the possibility of large profits associated with selling of crack, gangs worked hard to control their share of the market, and to expand their sales, territories, and profits.

Although not all scholars of gangs and their activities believe that there is a close association between gang homicides and drug trafficking, there is considerable evidence to support the view that these two forms of criminal activity are definitely interrelated. As one scholar who reviewed the body of available research concludes:

> Drug trafficking is an indirect contributor to youth gang homicide. The existence of gang drug markets provides a context in which gang homicides are more likely to occur. Because most youth gang homicides involve intergang conflicts, drug markets bring rival gang members into proximity with one another, thus increasing the likelihood of homicide. ... Although gang drug trafficking does not necessarily cause violence, gang participation, drug trafficking, and violence overlap (Howell, 1999, pp. 226–227).

One study of gang homicides over a five-year period in St. Louis has shown that gang homicides directly connected to drug trafficking tend to involve multiple victims, and have multiple witnesses in relation to gang homicides not directly connected to drug trafficking (Brandt and Russell, 2002). When a homicide is committed by a gang member who is not directly connected with drug trafficking activities, it is more likely to involve multiple perpetrators. One interesting facet of gang homicides that both does and does not tie directly to drug trafficking activity is that those homicides that are directly connected to drug trafficking are more likely to occur during the winter, whereas nondrug-connected gang homicides are more likely to occur during the spring and summer. This corresponds with the research findings that nearly all (86.7 percent) of drug trafficking-related gang homicides occur outdoors (where trafficking activities are almost always carried out), whereas gang homicides not directly tied to drug trafficking are likely to occur in a residence or a business. Other researchers, in other cities, also have shown that gang homicides are significantly more likely to occur outdoors, rather than in a residence or business (Klein and Maxson, 1989).

Gang homicides, statistically speaking, are actually less likely to be tied to the drug trade, which is in direct opposition to most assumptions about gangs and homicide. Perpetrators of gang homicides that are directly connected to drug trafficking tend to have prior offense records, to have drugs on them when they commit their offense, and to use semiautomatic guns in the killing (Brandt and Russell, 2002). Also, individuals killed in gang homicides directly connected to drug trafficking activities are more likely to be gang members themselves as compared with victims in gang homicides not directly connected to drug trafficking.

Conclusion

Homicides involving gang members are a relatively common form of homicide in the United States, especially in large cities. The proportion of homicides in the United States that are linked to gang members—as perpetrators, victims, or both—became a major crime concern in the past two to three decades. Although popular assumptions and fears about gang homicide may be exaggerated and not a true and significant threat for most Americans, nonetheless there is reason for many, especially inner-city, minority community members to be concerned.

Gang homicide is not a random event, nor something that eludes relatively easily identifiable patterns. When we look at who is involved, where such incidents tend to occur, and how such offenses are committed, we see very clear patterns. As summarized by Maxson (1999, p. 215), gang homicides "most often reflect the dynamics of gang membership, such as intergroup rivalries, neighborhood turf battles, identity challenges, and occasional intragroup status threats. The victims in gang homicides are usually other gang members." Gang homicides are an important crime issue in our society. Understanding the who, where, when, and how of such offenses is a worthy issue that deserves our attention.

Discussion Questions

1. What patterns distinguish gang homicide from other forms of homicide?
2. How is gang homicide related to other forms of crime in a community?
3. How has gang homicide changed in recent years, especially in regards to frequency and characteristics of who is involved and how killings occur?
4. How do the realities of gang homicide reflect and differ from popular beliefs and assumptions about gang activities?

Gangs and Police

3

Introduction

One fact that has been clearly shown throughout this book is that gangs have a number of negative effects on communities, community members, and the individuals who are gang members. Although there are some positive consequences of gang membership for some gang members, the negatives that arise from gangs are far more common. Most of these negative aspects of gangs are associated with the crimes that gang members commit. Therefore, gangs are an important issue that law enforcement agencies need to address. In order to make our communities safe and desirable places to live, the police need to be aware of gangs, work to keep individuals out of gangs, and effectively respond to the crimes committed and victims injured by gangs. Because gangs are involved in a variety of crimes, and sometimes a large number of crimes, it is important that police are aware of gangs, devote time and energy to prevent gangs from forming, and effectively respond to the harm gangs bring to communities.

In some ways, gangs and gang crimes are very similar to all forms of crime and criminals for which police have to respond. When community members are assaulted or threatened, when drugs are sold, when individuals are coerced into joining a gang, and when community residents are fearful of leaving their homes, it is the responsibility of the police to intervene, apprehend offenders, and return the community to a safe place. However, as we know from other discussions in this book, there also are important differences between "regular" crime and criminals and gangs and their offenses. Because of these differences, there is also a need for law enforcement authorities to respond, both proactively and reactively, in different ways when gangs are present and committing criminal offenses. Perhaps the most basic and, therefore, also highly important difference in how the police respond to gangs from other forms of crime and criminals is that, when dealing with gangs, it is critically important for the police to have a thorough understanding of who are the individuals in gangs, how and why youths join gangs, and what positive aspects members derive from being members. In order to do more than simply investigate a gang crime after it occurs, the police need to have intelligence about gangs and use that information to structure and implement coordinated responses to gangs. It is the way that police should coordinate their efforts and act to quell gangs and their criminal activities that is at the core of this chapter.

Police Response to Gangs

Identifying gangs and gang members, focusing efforts on monitoring gang members' activities, and responding to illegal activities of such persons is what is at the foundation of any police response to gangs. Gangs are an important issue for law enforcement agencies in most urban communities. Gang members are responsible for a significant portion of crime in many cities and, therefore, must be addressed by the police. However, while gangs and their activities are important to law enforcement agencies and officials, they are not necessarily considered the most important concern for most police agencies. Other types of offenders and offenses, such as property crimes, domestic violence, and drugs are typically more common problems, and, hence, also a higher priority for urban police (Kuhns, Maguire, and Cox, 2007). Emphases on nongang crime is especially strong in smaller cities and rural communities. This is not to say that gangs are not present and problematic in places other than major cities; gangs are present throughout American society. However, the time, effort, and resources devoted to the "gang problem" is significantly less of a priority in small cities, suburbs, and rural communities.

Law enforcement responses to gangs take two forms: prevention and intervention/suppression. Prevention activities typically focus on either efforts to prevent youth from joining gangs or preventing gangs and their members from engaging in criminal activities. Intervention and suppression activities are those efforts to quell gangs and to respond to their criminal activities in ways that control them and (hopefully) prevent ongoing criminal activities. Although most American cities today report the presence of gangs and gang-perpetrated crime, it is important to note that the specifics of gang activities vary across jurisdictions. Therefore, the specific ways that police in different cities act to prevent, intervene with, and suppress gang activities also vary significantly (Weisel and Painter, 1997).

Regardless of the specific ways that police respond to gangs and whether prevention or intervention is the focus of any agency or effort, a critical prerequisite for success is gathering and analyzing accurate information about gangs, their activities, their members, and the geographic/physical areas in which they operate. Without intelligence about gang members, their activities, where gang activities are more or less common, and the types of activities gang members engage in, it is unlikely that police will be very effective in their efforts. Knowledge is important and is critical for the development and implementation of all law enforcement efforts targeting gangs and gang activities.

Whatever specific form the response of a law enforcement agency takes, it is always important that such responses target those who are actually involved, likely to become involved, and that the response be more than simply trying to stop whatever gang activities are occurring at the current time. Rather, "the basic premise for any prevention and intervention efforts seems to be that programs must be targeted at providing at-risk and gang-involved youth with legitimate alternatives for fulfilling their basic needs, such as love, discipline, structure, belonging, personal safety, and protection. In other words, any gang-reduction or prevention program must include support and counseling for youths and their families (especially for hard-to-reach families and communities), education and training for youth toward earning an honest livelihood, and building skills for conflict resolution" (Chatterjee, 2007, p. 2).

The efforts of law enforcement agencies include both the actions of individual officers identifying and responding to gangs on their assigned beats or in the offenses they investigate, and creating and operating specialized gang units. When individual officers or detectives respond to gangs and their criminal offenses, there is little difference in how such officers respond to any crimes for which they are responsible. Although gang members may be involved, there remains the need to investigate what happened, how, and who was involved. Once this information is collected, the focus shifts to apprehending the individuals involved and moving the offenders through the criminal justice system. In these instances, the need for intelligence about gangs may not be as critical as it is for specialized units focusing all of their efforts on controlling gangs in the community.

Police Gang Units

Specialized units or departments within law enforcement agencies that are charged with the mission of monitoring gangs and responding to gang activities/crimes are common today in large cities. The first gang units in police departments were established in the United States in the late 1970s. By the early 1990s, the units had become common in large cities, with the period of 1990 to 1994 being the most active period for the creation of such units (Katz and Webb, 2004). This is to be expected, though, for the early 1990s saw a significant increase in violent crime in the United States, with much of the increase attributed (by scholars, the media, and some law enforcement officials) to gangs. In 1992, 90 percent of American cities with a population of 100,000 or more officially reported that they had a "gang problem" (Curry, Ball, and Fox, 1994). Therefore, the development of a specialized, focused response to an emerging public safety concern is not at all surprising. Additionally, the 1990s were a time when the basic management and organizational features of police departments were changing. This was a time when the movement away from police officers being "generalists" that addressed all forms and types of community problems was common, and accompanied by the creation of specialized units to address a number of issues (e.g., domestic violence, auto theft, child abuse, etc.).

To the public, gang units in police departments are seen as having been created out of a need for intensive efforts to control and eliminate gang crime, especially violent crime. In many cases, however, there is evidence that these units are the result of political and media attention to gang violence, and a police department perceiving that they need to respond to these political pressures (Katz and Webb, 2004). In at least some cities, gang units have been created in an attempt to quell nega-tive publicity, even when the objective reality of the "gang problem" has been small (Katz and Webb, 2004). In most communities when gang units are formed in police departments, they begin with a heavy emphasis on responding to violent crimes and working to suppress gang activities. However, once in place and operating, it is common for the activities of gang units to broaden, encompassing more than simply responses to offenses known or suspected to have been perpetrated by gang members (Weisel and Painter, 1997).

Gang units in police departments are primarily focused on four types of activities: intelligence gathering, investigations, suppression, and prevention (Weisel and Shelley, 2004). The intelligence gathering activities of gang unit officers are of two general varieties. First, these units and officers are involved in gathering information about individuals and groups who are believed to be associated with gangs, and monitoring the activities of known and suspected gangs. The second type of intelligence gathering is case-specific, in which officers are interested in learning about particular gangs' organization and activities, often with covert surveillance of and contact with gang members.

The investigative focus of police gang units is third and it follows typi-cally one of two forms: reactive and proactive. Reactive investigations are those that involve officers investigating crimes that have been committed with an emphasis (like police investigations in general) on identifying and apprehending offenders. Proactive investigations are those efforts in which gang unit officers focus their time and efforts on learning about large-scale, organized, and on-going criminal activities of gangs (Weisel and Shelley, 2004). The investigative activities of gang units are those efforts that are most focused on suppression of gangs, although it is an after-the-fact type of sup-pression that is desired or achieved.

Interestingly, the "prevention" activity that gang units engage in is fourth and it is typically not about preventing youth from becoming gang members. Instead, the prevention activities are focused on preventing gangs and gang members from committing crimes (Weisel and Shelley, 2004). It appears that prevention activities emphasizing keeping youth from joining a gang are usually a very low priority, if present at all, for law enforcement agency gang units. Interviews with gang unit officers reveal that prevention activities are among their lowest priority tasks (Katz and Webb, 2004). Such efforts are typically left to other units of a police department.

A fifth focus of many police department gang units, and one that is often overlooked or forgotten by those who study or work with police departments, is data management and analysis (Weisel and Shelley, 2004). This type of effort, in which gathered intelligence is organized and maintained for reference by (hopefully) all law enforcement officers, is not unique to gang units. Rather, in today's era of "intelligence lead policing," the collection of information about crimes, their location, individuals involved, characteristics, and location or movement within a community is a core principle of contemporary policing. For a police department gang unit, it is important to create, maintain, update, and regularly consult such databases and analyses of trends and changes in gang activities (including locations of activities) so as to support the investigation, suppression, and prevention activities that are at the core of the unit's mission.

Police officers and units dedicated to addressing gang issues are most common in urban or suburban areas. In rural communities, gangs, while certainly present, are not as serious or common a concern as they are in more populated communities. Across the United States, when looking at the crime and safety issues that are priorities for rural law enforcement agencies, gangs are low ranked issues (Kuhns, Maguire, and Cox, 2007). Consequently, law enforcement agencies in smaller communities are not likely to allocate resources (personnel, time, and money) to the issue of gangs. This fact is reinforced by the fact that in 2002 in Canada (a primarily rural nation), just over one-third (35 percent) of law enforcement agencies reported that they had a dedicated gang unit or gang officers. It is interesting to note that the majority of these units and officers are focused on intervention efforts; only 14 percent of Canadian law enforcement agencies report having any officers dedicated to gang prevention efforts (Royal Canadian Mounted Police, 2007).

At least in some cities, gang units may be hindered in their efforts by a lack of understanding of the true nature of gangs and their activities (Braga, McDevitt, and Pierce, 2006), as well as a lack of direction for and accountability of activities of these officers (Katz and Webb, 2006). At least in some law enforcement agencies, gang units operate with relative autonomy within the agency and have only minimal accountability to other units or superiors in the agency. This loose connection to the larger agency also may mean that the activities of gang units may at times function either in opposition or contrary to the efforts of the larger agencies. According to Katz and Webb (2006), this lack of connection to the larger organization may be most problematic for police departments that emphasize community policing. In such an instance, when the larger agency is focusing on establishing community partnerships, working with residents and businesses to identify concerns and problems and emphasizing the police as members of the community rather than simply a force responsible for controlling the community, the actions of gang units can be seen as not only failing to achieve the same goals, but perhaps also limiting the ability of police to be seen as partners. When gang unit officers are perceived as "hard" or only concerned with suppression of gang activities, the achievement of "partnerships" may be seriously inhibited.

However, not all studies support the idea that gang units are necessarily contrary to the goals of community policing. When there are carefully planned and implemented strategies, and ongoing communications between gang unit officers/leaders and others within the police department, gang units can actually be an important component of a community policing approach (Weisel and Shelley, 2004). One of the more important aspects of having an agency's gang unit complementing, rather than contradicting, the agency's overall focus is for there to be two-way sharing of information (e.g., communications) between the unit and other units and leaders of the department. Also important here is for the gang unit to have a focus and emphasis that is broader than the typical gang unit emphasis on suppression or intervention. Prevention activities and working with community members to keep youth from gangs is important for building and enhancing community partnerships, and for maintaining community trust, respect, and cooperation with the police.

One rather simple issue that is important for how well a gang unit communicates, shares information with, and integrates to the overall mission and activities of a police department is where the gang unit is located within a police department. Location is important in two ways, physical presence and where the unit is in the agency's organizational chart (which determines to whom the unit reports and by whom they are supervised). Some gang units are located in an agency's headquarters, housed alongside other specialized units and a detective bureau. Some gang units are centered out of a police substation in an area of the city where gang crime is considered most problematic. More common is for the gang unit to be housed in a secret, unmarked, away-from-other-police location (Katz and Webb, 2004). This approach is considered important by many departments so that the officers of the gang unit are less likely to be identified as police officers, which is important to facilitate their intelligence gathering work.

Placement of the gang unit within the organizational chart of a police agency is important for establishing accountability and lines of supervision. According to Katz and Webb (2004), there is a great deal of variability in where gang units are located within the organization. In some departments, the gang unit is administratively housed in the patrol division. In other departments, the gang unit can be found in Investigation, Special Investigations, a violent crime investigations unit, an intelligence unit, or alongside organized crime investigators. It should be clear that where a gang unit is placed in an organization will have at least some significant impact on who the officers interact and communicate with, as well as (at least symbolically) communicating to the members of the gang unit, the police department as a whole, and perhaps to outside community members, how much of a priority the unit and its work is.

Gang Unit Officers

The public's perception is that gang unit officers should have certain characteristics. The perception is that police officers working in gang units need to be younger, aggressive officers who are intimately familiar with the culture, backgrounds, and lifestyles of gang members. In their study of police gang units, Katz and Webb (2004) found that the characteristics of officers working in gang units were a reflection of characteristics of officers across the entire police department in which the unit was located. Perhaps the one characteristic that is skewed in the population of gang unit officers is sex: The vast majority of police gang unit members in the United States are men (however, keep in mind that across the nation women account for only approximately 12 percent of all police officers [National Center for Women and Policing, 2002]). Perhaps surprising to some, gang unit officers are typically in their 30s. Rather than gang unit officers "looking like" typical gang members, they tend to be officers with between 7 and 12 years of experience in law enforcement. One does not join the force and immediately become a member of the gang unit (despite what some movies and television shows might suggest). A position in an urban police department's gang unit is usually viewed by both gang unit officers and other officers as a high status job and one that is "a highly sought prize" (Katz and Webb, 2004, p. 253).

Not all observers see current police tactics for preventing or especially for intervening with gangs as positive, however. There are concerns that because many gangs have members who are all (or most) of one race or ethnicity, racial profiling occurs by the police in neighborhoods where the police believe gangs are operating (Duran, 2009). Both gang members and community residents who are not gang-involved, but are of the same race as the gangs in the community, may feel that law enforcement efforts are "too much" or "too strict" and operate on the assumption that all youths (especially young men) of the race in question are gang members and, consequently, all youth are targeted for police "monitoring." Interestingly, interviews with gang unit officers show some support for such an approach. "[G]ang unit officers perceived their units not as responding to *crime*, so much as responding to *groups of individuals* whom they believed to be deeply involved in criminal activities. Although this may be a fine distinction, it is meaningful. Gangs and gang members, not just their criminal acts, were viewed by the officers as the threat, and gang unit officers believed that their mission was to protect the community by combating those gangs" (Katz and Webb, 2004, p. 246). In such instances, it is easy, if not predictable, for gang unit officers to treat all similar-looking individuals as gang members, regardless of whether a specific individual is or is not gang involved. When community members perceive the police as profiling community residents and being too strict in their monitoring and intervention activities, resentment of the police is likely to be created or strengthened, with a breakdown in communications between police and community members, and, ultimately, law enforcement officers abusing their authority, albeit, in the pursuit of desired goals (Duran, 2009).

One of the most important aspects of any police–gang interaction is that it is critically important that gang members (or potential future members) perceive the police as respectful of youth. When youth believe that police are disrespectful of youth (either themselves or their peers), youth are significantly less likely to trust and respect the police in return, and more likely to believe it is acceptable to show disrespect to the police (Friedman, Lurigio, and Greenleaf, 2004). Such a situation makes it much more difficult for police to be effective in either prevention or intervention activities. Not surprisingly, gang-involved youth are more likely to report that they have been treated disrespectfully by the police than their nongang peers (Friedman, Lurigio, and Greenleaf, 2004).

Community Partners Working with Police

Responding to gangs in the community, especially in prevention efforts, are tasks that are most likely to be successful when the police have working relationships with other community members, groups, and agencies. Collaborating with other entities that can and do serve the same communities from which gangs come provides opportunities for prevention (and sometimes intervention) efforts to have a broader, deeper, and stronger reach. The types of partnerships that police efforts benefit from include schools, churches, public housing agencies, other criminal justice agencies (courts and corrections), businesses, and community social service organizations.

Community-based organizations, such as schools, churches, and nonprofit social service agencies, are important because they bring resources, perspectives, and skills that the police do not necessarily possess. The police are focused on responding to crime and, to some degree, preventing crime. The organizations that police work with in partnership are usually focused on addressing the social, financial, psychological, and mental health needs of community members. When the efforts directed at controlling and serving the needs of community members (including gang members) are combined into a coordinated set of efforts, there are obviously greater chances of success. And, in this context, success means enhanced community safety.

Creating and Sustaining a Successful Strategy to Address Gang Problems

Because the form and degree of gang problems in a community and the needs of communities vary across jurisdictions, there is not one specific way that is the best or most successful for law enforcement to address gangs and gang crime. A number of common characteristics, however, have been identified for how to create and sustain a successful response to gangs.

The first issue that almost all police departments advocate is to make sure that their efforts do not inadvertently encourage or promote gang activity. This point may seem self-evident, yet from experience many police departments have found that if they publicize their efforts, or even their successes, in responding to gangs, this information can have the effect of promoting gangs. Therefore, it is standard practice in most police departments not to report their efforts as "gang related." This means that not only do the police avoid naming their efforts as "gang response," but it also means that when discussing gang crime the police avoid providing the public (and the media) with names of gangs, individuals who are identified as gang members, and the names of victims of gang crimes. The belief here is that, if the police discuss gangs, they are serving to add to the notoriety of gangs. In this way, publicizing gangs and their activities can be seen as a form of advertising for the gangs. This is seen as counterproductive to the efforts of the police, and could result in increased recruitment for gangs and unnecessarily promoting fear among community members.

In addition to avoiding inadvertent encouragement or advertisement of gangs in a community, there also have been efforts of law enforcement agencies to identify sets of recommendations for how to address gangs and gang crime in a comprehensive manner. One of the most widely drawn upon and most complete sets of recommendations comes from the Royal Canadian Mounted Police. Based on a comprehensive review of the existing literature, experience in the community, and consultation with experts, the Royal Canadian Mounted Police (2007) have proposed a nine-step model for successfully combating gang activities. Their model includes:

1. Acknowledgment of the problem rather than denial is crucial to developing solutions.
2. An accurate and systematic assessment of the problem is very important.

3. Set goals and objectives based on a common understanding of the key concepts and the assessment of the problem. At the same time, focus on desired changes in the affected community.

4. The law enforcement community is well positioned to provide leadership in gang prevention and reduction efforts, and in coordinating a multiagency approach. It is important to establish a clear articulation with rationale of the assignment of responsibilities to each participating agency for relevant services and activities, and to coordinate these appropriately.

5. Strategies that combine prevention, intervention, and suppression components seem to be most effective in combating the gang problem. Providing youth—at-risk, gang-involved youth, and especially those who wish to leave gangs—with prosocial skills training, educational, and job opportunities for a healthy lifestyle must be an integral component of any prevention/intervention program.

6. Increasing awareness of gang problems toward prevention and counseling and support for effective intervention must be provided to the parents and teachers of at-risk and gang-involved youth. An effective gang prevention/intervention/suppression program should address all types of risk factors and try to provide the protective factors.

7. Consideration should be given to ongoing data collection through community-wide surveys, self-reports of youth and official records, monitoring and sharing of gang-related information. This would enable implementation of collaborative, interrelated strategies of formal (through strategic law enforcement and monitoring) and informal (community residents collaborating to maintain safety, order, and discipline) social control.

8. Adequate resources and their proper allocation are essential for such an initiative to be effective.

9. An evaluation component must be included so that knowledge on this important social issue can increase and contribute toward developing subsequent effective programs and strategies.

Conclusion

Law enforcement agencies devote significant amounts of time and energy to gangs and their crimes in their effort to maintain safe communities. Gangs can have serious negative consequences for communities, and the police are one of the primary agencies responsible for working to control gangs. The police focus most of their efforts against gangs on tasks of monitoring them, gathering intelligence about gang members and their activities, and working to both intervene in their activities and respond to the people that gangs victimize. Although preventing gangs from forming and recruiting new members are an important set of tasks, they tend to be lower priorities for the police than are the tasks of responding to gangs after they are in place and committing crimes.

One of the main ways that contemporary American law enforcement agencies work against gangs is through separate police gang units. These are sets of police officers who have the main responsibility for knowing about and working against gangs. Such units are usually organizationally separate from other units and departments of police departments, and composed of experienced officers who see their specialized job as high status and something worth competing for.

The police, however, should not be expected to control gangs by themselves. As is widely recognized in almost all aspects of policing, a coordinated response in which the police work with both other public service agencies and community organizations is likely to be the most effective form of response. As such, even though the police tend to focus their efforts on gang suppression, intervention, and prevention in specialized units of the agency, it is important that a community policing strategy be used when addressing gangs.

Discussion Questions

1. Discuss and explain how the ways that police respond to gangs and gang crime is different from the ways police respond to other types of crimes.
2. Explain and discuss the differences in a prevention and intervention approach by law enforcement to gangs.
3. What are the typical focuses of police gang units and how do the police fulfill these goals?
4. How are the police officers in gang units similar and how are they different from their peers who are not in gang units? How do the activities they perform as part of their job differ from those of traditional patrol officers?
5. What types of community organizations do police typically partner with in an attempt to combat gangs? Why do they partner with these organizations?
6. What are the major challenges and tasks involved in implementing a successful strategy to combat gangs?

Gangs and Schools

4

Introduction

At one time, schools were thought to be a place where parents would send their children to spend a better part of the day and learn in a safe and secure environment. Today, many schools and many communities are far from this, however. In some urban communities, schools closely resemble prisons with metal detectors, school resource officers (i.e., police officers), and crisis response drills (May, 2002). These features of schools are often thought to be necessary because of how schools are both products and reflections of the community and environment in which they are found. Simply put, the issues that take place in the community bleed into schools, just as what happens in schools impacts the community around the schools. One issue that seems to make its way into schools is the presence of gangs.

Gangs in schools may be disruptive to the school environment because their presence may result in several things, one of which may be fear. Students may be fearful to attend school and these fears, in turn, may result in students' poor academic performance. Another thing that may result from gangs' presence in schools is violence. Gangs may bring violence from the outside community into the school environment. The violence that occurs is likely to have detrimental effects on the students and the staff. With this said, it is clear that it is very important to understand the presence and consequences of gangs in our schools.

In this chapter, we will discuss the issues that social and behavioral researchers know about gangs in schools because it will provide some perspective and understanding of gangs in the school environment. Esbensen et al. (2010) have pointed out that gang researchers examine school factors less frequently than other factors. Before we may be able to understand the key issues of gang involvement in schools, it will be important to understand the extent of gangs in schools. Then, we will shift to understanding the motivations that individuals use to join a gang. Our next topic focuses on the problems that come with being in a gang in the school environment. Finally, this chapter will examine the issues of school violence and gang membership.

Extent of Gangs in Schools

One of the most important things to learn about gangs and schools is the extent to which gangs actually exist in schools. To understand this, a number of data sources need to be consulted. We discuss the two main data sources that are used in criminal justice and criminology: the Uniformed Crime Reports (UCR) and the National Crime Victimization Survey.

The UCR is maintained by the Federal Bureau of Investigation (FBI). The FBI receives its data from local law enforcement within the United States and it consists of the number of known crimes, arrests, and crimes that have been cleared. The data that are in the UCR may be used in at least two ways. First, the data may be arranged by the age of the offender allowing one to examine crime by juveniles and adults. Second, the UCR allows one to examine crime data in the context of rates. Rates are particularly useful because they provide an opportunity to understand the proportion of the population that has been arrested and whether this is higher or lower at any given time.

The UCR data are limited in several different ways. First, law enforcement tends to put all of the data together making it difficult to understand crimes by race/ethnicity, sex, age, or location. For instance, ethnicity is not always captured by the UCR. In the context of gangs, this would make it difficult to understand Hispanic, African-American, or Chinese gangs. In addition, it is difficult to know if the crimes that took place were in schools. Second, not all offenses that occur are known to law enforcement and, therefore, may not get included in the UCR. Also, some law enforcement agencies do not participate by sending their crime data to the FBI. As a result, we create what scholars sometimes refer to as the dark figure of crime—official statistics are not necessarily complete or completely accurate. Both of these contributing issues are among the reasons it is difficult to get information about the extent of gangs in schools.

Another data source is the National Crime Victimization Survey (NCVS). The NCVS is a nationally representative household survey that has been used to compare statistics on crime from other data sources, such as the UCR. This offers an opportunity to provide information about crime that has not been reported to the police. In addition, this is information that comes from a self-report format. Unfortunately, the NCVS has limits in that it provides victimization information, and this does not directly provide information about the extent of gangs in schools.

The self-report format, such as is used in compiling the NCVS, includes researchers who ask individuals to provide information about some event, attitude, or feeling. This has been a popular method of collecting data since Short and Nye's (1958) influential work on gangs. As highlighted in the NCVS, self-report data collection efforts allow the opportunity to capture information about the extent of gangs in schools that are not known to the police or that comes from victims. Thus, this sort of data may provide information about the extent of gangs in schools.

Beyond the two official data sources of the UCR and NCVS, there also are other, more focused datasets that can provide more valuable and more specific data about gangs in schools. The data that we use to explore the extent of gangs in schools comes from the National Center for Education Statistics (NCES). This organization has developed the Indicators of School Crime and Safety (2007) (http://nces.ed.gov/programs/crimeindicators/crimeindicators2010/). The responses used here are self-reports from students ages 12 to 18. This age range allows for students that are in sixth to twelfth grades to report (among a number of other issues) whether gangs were present in their schools during the previous six months.

In simple terms, gangs are present in our schools. In 2005, 24 percent of the students that were surveyed by the NCES indicated that gangs were present in their schools, and in 2007, 23 percent of the students believe that gangs were present in their schools. This may be an indication that the presence of gangs in schools is decreasing, but the decrease should not be considered to be large, or perhaps not even real. A one-percentage point drop in the perception of gangs in schools may be attributed to several different things. For one thing, the students that were surveyed may not have witnessed issues that would signal gangs in schools. Secondly, the students that were surveyed may not be completely truthful in completing the survey due to fear that may come from retaliation. An issue that arises with self-reports is that the survey participant may not be completely honest on the survey or may not have been in the "right" place at the "right" time to know of something's presence. Babbie (2002) explains that self-reports are an effective tool for collecting data on sensitive topics, but he also explains that not everyone that self-reports may be honest or aware. The one-percent change in the perception that gangs are present in schools may not be a substantial drop in the number or presence of gangs in schools. With these issues that are present about self-reports, it is important that we continue to look into the data to get a better picture of the extent of gangs in schools.

Next, we examine the extent of gangs in schools by sex. This allows us to understand better if males or females may perceive that gangs are present in their schools. In 2007, more males than females believed that gangs were present in their schools. Specifically, 25 percent of the males that were surveyed believed that gangs were present at their school, and 21 percent of the females believed that gangs were present at their school. This may occur because gang members are more likely to be males (Thompkins, 2000; http://nces.ed.gov/programs/crimeindicators/crimeindicators2010/) than females. Thus, gang members are more likely to reveal themselves to males than to females in an effort to recruit them into the gang. This does not mean that the gangs do not reveal themselves to the females, and the percentage of females perceiving that gangs are present in their schools suggests that this is the case.

The perception that gangs were present in schools also differs by race and ethnicity in the 2007 NCES report. The larger percentage of students that perceived that gangs were present in their schools came from those of color. For instance, 38 percent of the African-American students reported that they perceived that gangs were present in their schools. Of the Hispanic students, 36 percent reported that they perceived that gangs were present in their schools. The percentages for African-Americans and Hispanics were nearly two times higher than the percentages for whites and Asian students. Of the white students, 16 percent reported that that they perceived that gangs were present in their schools, and 17 percent of the Asian students reported the same. This may be a result of the concentration of the gangs in the African-American and Hispanic communities where students are drawn from for the school student population (Thompkins, 2000; http://nces.ed.gov/programs/crimeindicators/crimeindicators2010/); thus, these students know the members of the gangs from outside of the school environment. This may make them more likely to report that they perceive that gangs are present in their schools.

The perceived presence of gangs also differs by grade level. Students in lower/earlier grades reported less presence of gangs in schools. Specifically, the students that were in grades 6 through 8 (15 to 21 percent) reported that they perceived that gangs were present in their school at a lower rate than the students who were in grades 9 through 10 (24 to 28 percent). This would suggest that gangs are not revealing themselves to younger students or that younger students are less likely to be in settings and situations where gangs are present and visible.

The perception that gangs are present in school also differs by type of school. Students that attend public schools reported 20 percentage points higher than students that attend private schools that gangs were present in schools. This would suggest that the selective nature of private schools is likely to weed out students that may have knowledge of gangs; conversely, the students that attend public schools are much more likely to be around other students that are part of gangs (Joseph, 2008). Taken in total, these data provide a strong indication that gangs are part of the American school environment.

Motivations to Joining a Gang

In many ways, joining a gang is a process because it involves a decision and one or more situational components. An individual joins a gang based on a rational choice. At some level, the individual has decided that joining the gang would provide them more of a benefit than a cost. The important focus here is to determine the mechanisms that may motivate the individual to assess the decision of joining a gang in this manner.

The neighborhood in which the individual lives and the school that the individual attends are mechanisms that may motivate the individual to join a gang. Youth who live in communities characterized by social disorganization may have environmental factors present in their lives that may motivate them to join a gang. For instance, if the neighborhood is a high crime area, gangs are much more prevalent, and this allows the individual to be socialized into a gang (Wyrick and Howell, 2004). Moore (1998) argued that neighborhoods that do not have effective forms of adult supervision and, thus, allow youth to have a substantial amount of free time are ripe for individuals to join gangs. In addition, disorganized neighborhoods usually do not create opportunities as adults for prosocial jobs. In these types of neighborhoods, gangs may be able to operate and congregate without incident or provocation (Moore, 1998). Researchers have supported these neighborhood reasons for joining a gang (Gottfredson and Gottfredson, 2001; Howell, 2003; Wyrick and Howell, 2004).

The neighborhood is the larger environment in which the school operates. A socially disorganized neighborhood is likely to have gangs in the schools. The students that the school serves are going to be the residents from the neighborhoods; thus, when the disorganization of the neighborhood is a reason that an individual joins a gang, then schools are likely to have the presence of gangs. Despite the neighborhood being socially disorganized, this in itself may not be enough of a motivation to push youth to join a gang; in fact, other neighborhood factors may serve as the impetus for an individual to join a gang.

The gang member joins because the gangs are present and known within a neighborhood or a school. To show that the individual belongs to the neighborhood, he will join the gang to prove a commitment to the neighborhood. In Hispanic neighborhoods, some gangs have been around for many decades; thus, gang membership may be seen as a form of patriotism. The patriotism is important to the residents of the neighborhood because generations of gang members may be present there. To fit in with the rest of the neighborhood, the individual may join a gang. The same may be said about a particular school. That is, individuals who attend a specific school may be expected to join a gang. The gang becomes a tradition in the school and the school is the "turf" in which the gang operates. Regardless of whether it is the neighborhood or school, the larger environmental structure is important for individuals to decide to join a gang, but individual motivators for joining a gang are important as well.

Individual motivators may shape the decision to join a gang. One motivator is money and employment. Most individuals that join gangs believe that joining a gang will relieve them from financial poverty. Gangs usually perform illegal acts to earn money for their activities. One of the most common forms of employment for a gang is selling drugs, and this activity may be very lucrative. In fact, the money that a gang member may earn from selling drugs may be more than he would ever make in a legitimate job.

Another motivator is the entertainment that comes from gang activity. Gangs usually provide an environment that is not different than a fraternity, sorority, or lodge (e.g., Kentucky's Oleka Shriners). In recreation, gangs are active. One of the activities that comes with gang life is partying. The parties are often supplied with drugs and the spoils of illegal activity provide the money to finance the party. Some boys and young men join gangs to meet women. The probability of meeting women, once an individual is a gang member, likely increases because the gang member is able to enjoy a certain amount of status, thus, providing entertainment.

Some join gangs because it provides the member with an opportunity to hide along with a source of protection. Gang members may need to hide from others or the police. Given the potential neighborhood that the gang member may live in, the gang may provide a refuge from the police and others. The same may be true when it comes to gangs in school. Gangs provide a safe haven from school officials allowing the gang member to be away from school.

Individuals join gangs because of the certain danger that exists in their neighborhoods and schools. In low-income, socially disorganized neighborhoods, the number of predators is vast because they are seeking income to improve their situations. Gang membership provides a form of protection from these predators that allows the individual to pursue ventures, usually illegal ventures. Researchers have shown that some gang members previously had been victims (Esbensen et al., 2010; Joseph, 2008; Thompkins, 2000), and that their gang participation was an effort not to be victimized again. The protection does not stop in the neighborhood. The cloak of protection from gangs makes its way into the school environment (and, as discussed in Chapter 11, even jail and prison). Gang members that were victims in school were less likely to be a victim in the school environment after joining the gang.

Some join gangs because they are rebelling from their parents or guardian. Researchers have shown that some join gangs so that they do not become like their parents (Esbensen et al., 2010; Joseph, 2008). Their parents are usually unemployed, underemployed, or working a job in a secondary market that has a dead end (i.e., manual labor). Gang membership marks a stance that the gang member is not going to participate in these sorts of (demeaning? unrewarding?) jobs. The illegal markets where gangs operate their businesses are much more lucrative and the money comes in faster than from the jobs that their parents have. Therefore, joining a gang is an effort to improve the gang member's living conditions.

Joining a gang is a combination of these factors that may distort the perception of the benefit or cost of gang membership. Researchers have shown that joining a gang is a well thought out decision that is driven by what the individuals see as being in their best interest. Joining a gang does not occur on a whim and is a process that needs to be understood so that it is feasible to understand gangs in schools.

Gang Recruitment

While joining a gang may be a decision that is influenced by neighborhood, school, and individual factors, we also need to remember that gangs do actively recruit some of their members. This just means that gangs are seeking out new members. New gang members may be brought in to the gang in two primary ways.

One technique that is used for recruitment is a testing format. In an approach that is very similar to fraternity or sorority rush/recruitment, a gang may throw a party so that the gang members and the potential recruit may meet to size each other up. The new recruit is evaluated based on their ability to fight, courage, and ability to assist other gang members. The main criterion in these parties is to evaluate the new recruit's potential or ability to fight. If the new recruit's ability to fight is known, then no additional testing is likely to be necessary. However, if it is unknown, then the new recruit may be tested to determine his ability to fight. In the school environment, such social events do not occur, but fights may occur to test the new recruit. Testing the new recruit provides the current gang members an opportunity to assess how well he will protect and stand up for the gang in a public manner. In addition, this places an emphasis on the new recruit needing a place to hide from school officials or law enforcement. In other words, the new recruit tests occurring at school create additional conditions where the new recruit will need the gang even more.

Another potential recruitment technique is using the sense of duty. Some gangs will work to convince a new recruit that it is his duty to join a gang. This form of gang recruitment occurs in neighborhoods and schools that have a long tradition of gangs. The duty form of recruitment is effective for potential recruits that value being respected in the neighborhood or schools, and fear losing that respect.

Effects of Gang Membership and School Gang Affiliation

Gang membership may have substantial long-term consequences for the gang member. Researchers have examined the effect that gang membership may have on an individual. In this section, we discuss some of these issues.

Decker and Van Winkle (1996) argued that joining a gang is an important turning point in the life of gang members. Joining a gang places the individual into a situation where they may experience negative effects in adulthood. Short (1989) argued that gangs do not develop or exercise the skills necessary to function in conventional settings, including schools. Gang life operates counter to many of the norms and requirements of prosocial life. As mentioned above, individuals often join gangs for protection, may have been recruited because they were good fighters, and their degree of being streetwise is valued (Short, 1989). Put differently, Rand (1987) argued that gang membership delays the maturation from adolescence to adulthood.

The effects of gang membership begin with deviant behavior. Fifty years ago, Yablonsky (1962) showed that criminal and deviant behavior increased when an individual joined a gang. This is important because it is used to evaluate the loyalty and value of a gang member to the gang. In other words, for a gang member to move up in the hierarchy of the gang (and, therefore, gain more rewards), he has to perform criminal and deviant acts. The deviant acts that gangs produce often bleed over into the school environment.

This puts the gang member at risk with school administration and teachers, who may focus their monitoring and discipline on gang members. Focusing on the gang members means that their behaviors will become known more often than the deviant/criminal behaviors of those who are not gang members. The additional effect of so much attention is that teachers are likely to label gang members as "bad" or disturbed (Esbensen et al., 2010). The label may be real or imagined, but it is something that is likely to follow the gang member throughout their time in school. This makes the behavior of a gang member much more scrutinized by teachers.

The scrutiny does not stop with the teachers, but also moves into the purview of administrators, who are likely to be aware of gang members' activities because of their label of being bad or disturbed. The behaviors that gang members exhibit are much more likely to lead to more suspensions and expulsions (Joseph, 2008; Thompkins, 2000). The suspensions and expulsions create additional issues. Hemphill et al. (2006) argued that removing the gang members from school is really removing them from adult supervision and, therefore, increasing the opportunity for more association with delinquent peers and delinquency. Thus, the additional knowledge of gang members' activities may make them much more likely to become more entrenched into gang life because they are often suspended and expelled from school.

Beyond behavioral and labeling issues, gang membership has academic implications as well. Thornberry and Krohn (2003) showed that poor performance on math tests is linked with gang membership. One way that this may work is that those that are not interested in what is necessary to perform well on math tests may suggest problems with tenacity that could lead to gang membership. Another way is that math tests represent prosocial logic and thought processes; as mentioned above, these thought processes are generally rejected by potential gang members. Thus, gang members are not likely to perform well on math tests.

Math test performance is not the only academic issue that affects gang membership. Thornberry and Krohn (2003) argued that academic aspirations, low attachment to teachers, low college expectations from parents for their child, and low degree of school commitment are other school-related issues that affect gang membership. Given that gang members seem to be interested in earning fast income and gaining immediate status, academic aspirations do not seem to be in the forefront of gang members' lives. The ability to survive in life in the neighborhood or a school through gang life is much more important than academic aspirations.

Gang members, not surprisingly, also do not seem to be as committed to school as nongang members (Esbensen et al., 2010; Bjerregaard and Smith, 1996; Esbensen and Deschenes, 1998; Maxson, Whitlock, and Klien, 1998). Esbensen et al. (2010) showed that gang members had a significantly lower level of commitment than nongang members. The nongang members were much more likely to try hard in school as opposed to the gang members, especially in areas of homework (Esbensen et al., 2010). The lack of commitment makes sense given that the gang member is motivated by money and employment. A gang member is likely to view the (illicit) opportunity to make several thousand dollars in a short amount of time as much more seductive than school and homework.

Gang membership also seems to influence an individual's perception of limited educational opportunities. Esbensen et al. (2010) reported that gang members saw more limited educational opportunities than nongang members. This feeds into the idea that gang members who do not have a commitment to school and the tenacity to complete their homework are not likely to see a future in the academic arena. This may suggest to them that they are not going to be able to obtain high quality and high paying jobs in legitimate markets. In addition, the work ethic and time necessary to change these views does not provide the immediate gratification of money and status that many gang members seek. With this in mind, it seems that gang members will see their educational opportunities limited because they are not able to achieve the types of employment that they desire in the legitimate markets, and devoting time and energies to educational activities reduces their opportunities to earn money fast.

These social indicators of the effects of gang membership are important, but they do not cover physical effects that may take place. Victimization among gang members occurs more than among nongang members (Laub and Lauritsen, 1998; Esbensen et al., 2010). This does occur within the school environment as well. However, the level of gang membership victimization is not clear cut according to Joseph's (2008) results. She showed that more gang members (14 percent) than nongang members (10 percent) were victims of assault with a weapon in school, but fewer gang members (2 percent) were robbed at school than nongang members (7 percent). Regardless of Joseph's disparate results, it is clear that victimization is one of the effects for gang members at school.

Few will argue that the gang environment is dangerous, and, as mentioned above, some join gangs because they are seeking refuge from danger. The danger may be in the neighborhood, but some researchers have shown that gang members perceive the school environment as being dangerous. For example, Esbensen et al. (2010) showed that gang members see their school environment as being hostile and unsafe. This could be because rival gangs also may attend the same school. If rival gangs attend the school, this increases the likelihood of fights or other forms of fear-invoking activity (e.g., intimidation) (Thompkins, 2000). In addition, schools are within neighborhoods. If the neighborhood has a gang problem, the likelihood of these problems coming into the schools increases (Thompkins, 2000). For those that are gang members, they may recognize these problems sooner than those that are not gang members.

Gangs and School Violence

While the attention to violence at school has increased due to some celebrated cases (e.g., Columbine, Paducah, and Virginia Tech), these incidents cannot be blamed on gang activity. This does not mean that gang activity does not play an influential role in some of the violence that takes place in schools. From above, the development of gangs does not happen magically or overnight. Gangs are the result of poor community and ineffective family environments. When these environments are not able to sustain economic prosperity and stable families, crime and gang activity seem to increase (Jackson, 1991; Padilla, 1992). Schools are not inoculated from this sort of activity and can be influenced by this; thus, gangs may become part of the school and its culture. Once this happens, violence will become a reality. Here, we discuss the extent of gang violence in schools and point out some potential reasons for this behavior.

Huff (1998) studied 100 students in four separate cities. Of these students, in each city, 50 were gang members and 50 were not gang members, but were at-risk youth. Huff asked the gang and nongang members about their behavior in school. His study revealed that selling drugs and violence were performed in school by both gang and nongang members. While selling drugs is important, the key issue in this section is violence. Huff showed that 51 to 58 percent of the gang members reported that they assaulted students, which is a higher percentage than for nongang members (35 percent).

This suggested that gang members are much more violent than nongang members. While Huff's study is more than a decade old, other researchers have performed similar studies and have supported his findings. For instance, Howell and Lynch (2000) studied gangs in school and found that gangs were involved in drug sales and violence just as Huff had shown.

Knox (2006) performed a study of K–12 students to understand the extent of gang activity in schools. Over 40 percent (42 percent) of the students indicated that gang fights had occurred in schools in the previous year. This supports the Huff (1998) and Howell and Lynch (2000) results that gang members were involved in assaults. Knox went on to show that 12 percent of the students indicated that they had been threatened with gang-related violence at school. A staggering finding from Knox was that 26 percent of the students reported that gang-related shootings took place near their schools supporting the notion that the violence outside of schools tends to influence the school environment.

Joseph (2008) used data from students attending two secondary schools to examine the extent of violence in schools due to gang membership. Her results showed that more gang members (48 percent) hurt someone in school compared to nongang members (21 percent). In addition, more gang members (39 percent) than nongang members (11 percent) participated in fights. This supports the notion that gang members were more likely to take part in assaults that nongang members.

Other important findings are necessary to address in the context of violence in schools: weapons in schools. That is, gang members are much more likely to bring weapons to school and to use these weapons than nongang members. We return to Huff's (1998) study that showed that more gang members (38 to 58 percent) than nongang members (10 percent) brought knives to school. Huff noted that more gang members (40 to 53 percent) compared to nongang members (10 percent) admitted to carrying guns to school. This supports the view that gang members are more likely than nongang members to bring weapons to school. While this study provides some indication of gang members bringing weapons to school, the study is limited because it is over a decade old. To update Huff's (1998) research, Joseph (2008) showed that gang members (18 percent) were more likely to assault someone in school with a weapon than nongang members (2 percent). This research supports the overall notion that weapons in school due to gangs does occur and that the weapons are being used in our schools.

The issue of violence in schools because of gangs is a major concern (Joseph, 2008). The natural question that may arise is why this may occur. The reasons for typical gang violence and motivations to join gangs may provide some basic insight into this problem. Here, we follow Thompkins' (2000) lead and put these into perspective. To clarify, Thompkins argued that the gang violence problems came from the "us against them" mentality that the administration tends to take when faced with gang problems. The "us against them" mentality tends to have some unfortunate potential effects. One is the "bad boy syndrome." This is where the "us against them" mentality pushes the student into the gang because he wants to be seen as an outsider that disobeys the rules and is dangerous. Another potential effect is competition. The "us against them" mentality makes some space in the schools and respect in the schools competitive and gangs become violent to earn one or the other. The next effect is "special person." The "us against them" mentality singles out gang members and gives them more attention. Consequently, making them "special" to the others in the school may actually have the effect of making their personas desirable.

Conclusion

Few will argue with the view that gangs are within our schools. The extent of gang activity in our schools, however, is not very well known. From the available data, more males and students of color are attending schools with gangs. Individuals often join gangs because of a commitment to their neighborhood. Some also join gangs for money, entertainment, protection, and/or rebellion against authority figures. Gang membership comes with several important consequences: poor academic performance, lack of skill development, deviant and criminal behavior, and victimization. Violence by gangs is an important issue in schools. Gangs then are not just present in our schools, but they are disruptive to the entire school environment as well.

Discussion Questions

1. Explain the reasons for the problems with understanding the extent of gangs in schools.
2. What are the characteristics of someone who would join a gang?
3. Discuss why someone would join a gang out of allegiance to his neighborhood.
4. Explain how gang problems in neighborhoods come into the schools.

Motorcycle Gangs 5

Introduction

Particularly since the end of World War II, motorcycle clubs and motorcycle gangs have been a part of our American culture. The names of these gangs are well-known to most: the Mongols, the Hell's Angels, the Pagans, the Outlaws, and the Bandidos. What often started as social and drinking groups has moved into crimes of all types including murder, rape, drugs, smuggling, kidnapping, and prostitution (Richardson, 1991). Some of these gangs developed after the Korean and the Vietnam Wars when the veterans came home from battles abroad only to be greeted by less than enthralled groups at home. Finding others of a similar ilk, many joined together in the pursuit of self-interests and solutions of common concerns. Many of these interests centered on drugs, the abuse of alcohol, and various crimes of violence ranging from mugging to murder.

What we intend to show in this chapter is the history of several individual gangs, their main members, and their goals and viability. While most gang members are law-abiding, there are the "1%ers," the 1 percent of the gang population who intentionally commit crimes and, thus, become involved with the criminal justice system (Finlay and Matthews, 1996).

America's Motorcycle Gangs: A Brief History

After WWII, many motorcycle gangs became well-known, antisocial forces on the streets. While the majority of motorcycle gangs were social outlets for men returning from various global conflicts, as time passed, less emphasis was placed on the social outlets and more on criminal activities. This is no better illustrated than in the groups calling themselves the Hell's Angels (Allender, 2001) or the Bandidos (Rijn, Edwards, and Brennan, 2006).

Eight men of Toronto, Canada, were found dead in a home at a farm owned by a known member of a local biker gang, the Bandidos. The investigation was not certain if the killings were a result of a gang cleansing or if another motive was involved. One victim was a truck driver who was not a member of the gang, but cruised the highways in his tow truck to come to the aid of stranded motorists. The Outlaws have issued a statement denying any involvement in the killings (Rijn, Edwards, and Brennan, 2006).

51

The Bandidos and the Hell's Angel are not the only motorcycle gangs involved in trouble with the law. Thirty-seven Sons of Silence members were arrested in 1999 on charges of drug trafficking and illegal weapons in Denver, Colorado (http://findarticles.com/p/asrticles/mi_qn4191/is_1991009/ ai_9964034/). On Labor Day, 2004, two young girls, ages 14 and 15, were allegedly taken from their dates near the town of Seaside, California. When the girls were found several hours later, one girl was nude and the other had on only a torn sweater. Soon, four gang members of the Hell's Angels were arrested for rape, kidnapping, and other charges (Thompson, 2009). The Hell's Angels, located out of California, have been illustrated in movies, such as *The Wild One*, starring Marlon Brando, and *Easy Rider* with Peter Fonda and Jack Nicholson (Table 5.1).

In 1995, John Bartolomeo was sentenced to 35 years in prison for the murder of a member of the Devils Disciples motorcycle gang. In Massachusetts, he ran over "Cats" Michaels in his car in retaliation for dealing in drugs in his area, which the Hell's Angels considered their own turf (http://www.power-sportsnetwork.com/moptorcyclenewswsdetail/id=1255/newsarticle1255.htm (retrieved September 22, 2009).

The crimes of the Outlaws (Figure 5.1) and the Hell's Angels are not new. Trethewy and Katz (1998) stated that outlaw motorcycle gangs have had more than 50 years to hone their skills and become a major criminal force. These outlaw motorcycle gangs have outings to solidify their gang unity and also to congregate with other gang members to cooperate, plan, and carry out the criminal actions of their groups. Johnson (1981) reported that members of these two groups were involved in stealing Harley Davidson motorcycles and other motor vehicles for 30 years in North Carolina.

In 2002, many members of rival motorcycle gangs waged war inside Harrah's Casino in Laughlin, Nevada. The result? Three people were killed and 13 were taken to a local hospital with gunshot wounds and stab wounds. Witnesses said the two gangs involved in this fatal incident were the Mongols and the Hell's Angels (Bach, 2002). Mongol Anthony "Bronson" Barrera, 43, was stabbed to death and two Hell's Angels, Jeramie Bell (27) and Robert Tumelty (50), were shot to death (Bach, 2002).

Victims of violent physical and sexual crimes have a very difficult task in determining if the perpetrator was a gang member or not. In 90 percent of cases, a strict determination could not be made. Moreover, males were more likely to be victimized by gang members than females. Also, Hispanics were more likely to be able to identify their assailants as gang members (Miller, 2010).

In November 2007, Christopher Ablett, 37, an alleged member of the Mongols Motorcycle Club, was sought in San Francisco on charges of killing Mark "Papa" Guardado, the head of the Hell's Angels' "Frisco" chapter. Police

Table 5.1 Overview of American Motorcycle Gangs

Name of Motorcycle Gang	Location	Number of Members	Alleged Criminal Activities	Founded In	Allies with Gangs, Such As …	Rivals With Gangs, Such As …
Vacos	California	300	Drugs/Murders/Stolen property	1965	Hell's Angels	
Free Souls	Oregon	100	Drugs/Auto thefts/Arms dealings	1968	Vacos	
Bandidos	Texas	2500	Drugs/Murders/Stolen property	1966	Outlaws, Mongols	Hell's Angels, Sons of Silence
Highwaymen	Michigan	200	Drugs/Prostitutions/Murders/Racketeering	1954	Sons of Silence	Outlaws
Warlocks	Pennsylvania	500	Drugs/Murders/Burglarys/Kidnapping	1967	Hell's Angels, Sons of Silence	
Sons of Silence	Colorado	275	Drugs/Murders/Prostitution	1966	Highwaymen, Warlocks	Bandidos
Outlaws	Illinois	1700	Bombing/Murder/Prostitution	1935	Mongols, Pagans, Bandidos	Hell's Angels, Highwaymen
Pagans	Maryland	400	Murders/Extortions/Arsons/Prostitution	1959	Bandidos, Mongols, Outlaws	Hell's Angels, The Breed
Mongols	California	600	Illegal firearm sales/Murders/Drugs	1969	Hell's Angels, Free Souls	
Hell's Angels	California	3600	Racketeerings/Murders/Drugs	1948	Aryan Brotherhood	Pagans, Bandidos
Iron Horsemen	Ohio	Unknown	Drugs Prostitution	1965	Hell's Angels, Sons of Silence	Outlaws

Figure 5.1 The Outlaws' Patch: The "skull and pistons" along with the skull, the name of the club, and, finally, at the bottom, the location of the chapter. (From the FBI.)

believe Ablett shot Guardado, 46, after what police describe as a "wrestling match" outside a Mission District bar the night of September 2. Witnesses told police that the killer rode away on a motorcycle (Black, 2004).

In April 2008, hundreds of motorcyclists gathered in Eugene, Oregon, to celebrate the fortieth anniversary of the founding of the Free Souls Motorcycle Gang. Also in town for that event were members of the Mongols Motorcycle Gang, one of the most violent gangs in the United States. The police were faced with a potential homicidal problem. Although they were braced for anticipated violence, thankfully nothing of any major consequence occurred (Denson, 2008). Was this a new beginning? Hardly.

There have been several well-known persons who have belonged to motorcycle clubs. Jesse "The Body" Ventura was a well-known professional wrestler in the 1980s. After leaving the Navy Seals in 1973, he lived in San Diego, California, where he joined The Mongols, a 1%er motorcycle club. When asked if he had broken any laws with The Mongols, Ventura denied any involvement with breaking the law. Standing 6'4" and weighing 245 lbs., Ventura became an instant hit with the professional wrestling fans, often serving as an enemy of "Hulk" Hogan. He retired in 1984 after being on the professional wrestling circuit for nine years. In 1998, he ran successfully for governor in Minnesota, and, after his term, he returned as a TV personality for the wrestling networks (Ventura and Russell, 2009).

Biker Violence in Other Countries

Not surprising, biker violence is not restricted to the United States. The Royal Canadian Mounted Police report about 1,200 members of motorcycle gangs in Canada. In Canada, five bikers were arrested in a case of mass murder in 2006 in southeastern Ontario. Only recently, another past president of the Outlaws, Jeffrey LaBrash, was killed in a gun fight with members of other motorcycle gangs (The Associated Press, 2009).

In Germany, the Hell's Angels and the Bandidos have wreaked havoc on the countryside in that country. Deggerich and Stark (2009) report a long-standing history of hostility between the two gangs. This rivalry between the two gangs is extant also in the United States with one gang attacking the other, inflicting mayhem with the continued commission of violent crime.

In other parts of Europe, three motorcycle groups are dominant: the Hell's Angels, the Bandidos, and the Outlaws. These gangs are allegedly involved in crimes ranging from traditional drug smuggling to vehicle crimes to human trafficking and contract killings. They are spreading throughout the new member-states of the European Union, but are particularly active in the Nordic countries, Germany, and Belgium. They are becoming more active in Britain as well. The main gang activity in Europe is drug trafficking. Illegal substances enter the countries through several overland and sea routes, controlled by different gangs. For example, routes through the Nordic and Baltic regions are dominated by Russian-speaking gangs, while the Atlantic area is in the grip of the Dutch, the British, and the Belgians. These well-established routes also have become corridors for illegal immigration, alcohol, and other gangs that use their escape plans to leave undesirable sites. Tobacco smuggling and sex-slave trafficking are prevalent; regarding the latter, each year, more than 100,000 women and children are trafficked across Eastern European borders. Many end up in forced prostitution in brothels or on the streets of large urban areas. (Thompson, 1996).

Europe's Five Major Biker Gangs

1. The first is the **Outlaws.** The British offshoot of the world's most infamous motorcycle gang was born after two English bikers visited, and took their impetus from, its West Coast birthplace. The group, officially sanctioned in 1969, organized the "Bulldog Bash," one of the biggest biker events in Europe.

   The Outlaws had relatively modest beginnings in Illinois in 1935, and, by the turn of this century, the Outlaws had grown to encompass 200 chapters around the world. The British arm of the club came under the aegis of its New World forefathers in 2000, and currently boasts units in Birmingham, London, Kent, and the Forest of Dean. Members flaunt a crossed piston and skull motif on the back of their black leather jackets.

2. The **Blue Angels** started in Glasgow, Scotland. Its name derives from Scotland's national colors; some members state the "Blue" stands for bastards, lunatics, undesirables, and eccentrics. They began by using stripped-down Triumph/Norton hybrids (without lights) as their ride of choice. Chapters in Leeds and Sheffield first drove onto British roads in 1997.
3. **Road Tramps,** formerly known as the Grim Reapers, was established in Ireland in 1987. It is part of the Irish Motorcycle Club Alliance, an umbrella organization drawing together the Vikings, Freewheelers, and Devils Diciples (*sic*). The Road Tramps also have an English following in London and Liverpool.
4. **Bandidos'** slogan is: "We are the people your parents warned you about." They are estimated to have 2,400 members in 195 chapters across 14 countries and many states in the United States. The club, which originated in Texas, is among the Angels' fiercest and most violent rivals (Thompson, 2009).
5. In both Ireland and England, the **Devils Diciples** (*sic*) were originally founded in California in 1967. The Diciples (originally deliberately misspelled) developed into a criminal gang.

The crimes of these gangs seem to be originally centered on drugs and murder. However, we will see there are other crimes committed by the 1%ers.

Motorcycle Gangs in the United States: The Big Four

The Outlaws

Perhaps the most noted motorcycle gang in the United States is the Outlaws. Originally only a small group of military veterans joined after WWII; they were attracted to the Harley-Davidson motorcycle if for no other reason than they were made in the United States. Their goals centered on a sense of joined brotherhood and a dedication to personal freedom, and nonconformity to overall society's folkways, mores, laws, and institutions. Because of its propensity to crime, the American Motorcycle Association (AMA) does not sanction the group (Drew, 2002).

The command structure of the Outlaws is similar to that of many other bureaucracies. In the Outlaws, there is a president, vice president, treasurer, secretary, and sergeant at arms (Jones, 2001), not unlike many businesses operating in this country today. There are many 1%ers in the Outlaws who are dedicated to lives of crime, including robbery, extortion, and prostitution (Drew, 2002).

**ORGANIZATIONAL STRUCTURE OF THE
OUTLAW MOTORCYCLE GANG**

National President: Often the founder, elected by the gang itself.

Regional Representative: The national vice president.

National Enforcer: Bodyguard and answers directly to the president.

Chapter President: Head of a local unit and authority of all chapter business.

Chapter Secretary/Treasurer: Collects dues, takes minutes, responsible for finances.

Sergeant at Arms: In charge of maintaining order at club meetings.

Road Captain: Usually the security chief for sponsored runs or outings (Carlie, 2002).

Patches and Colors of the Outlaws

Not all Outlaws of 1% gangs called themselves members of the Outlaws club. They may have a different name but are still affiliated with the Outlaws in shared membership, ideologies, and goals. In other words, there are sets inside the general outlaw or 1% category. Each group will have a cloth patch that will identify the club to which the wearer belongs. Like street gangs mentioned in a previous chapter, motorcycle gangs will wear patches and clothing of different colors. For example, in some groups, the wearer may decorate his patch with the color green. This denotes that the wearer has had sex with a woman with venereal disease. Purple on his patch tells the viewer that he has had sex with a corpse. How true this is and how much it is intended to fool those outside the subculture of the gang is, however, open to debate (Pratt, 2006).

1%ers: Name given to motorcycle gang members who are considered "outlaws." The other 99 percent are considered to be law abiding and social.

The Relationships and Confederation of Outlaws

Periodically, representatives of outlaw motorcycle gangs will meet in a neutral area to discuss problems, issues, and disagreements that may exist among the various motorcycle gang units within that confederation. The diverse members of the various motorcycle gangs will try to resolve issues without violence and bloodshed. Of course, it stands to reason that the larger and the more powerful 1%er motorcycle gangs usually get their way with the smaller and less powerful gangs. And, usually the smaller groups exist at the whim and via support of the larger groups.

At times, some of the larger groups are at war with other large motorcycle gangs. This holds true, for example, with gangs such as the Outlaws, the Mongols, and the Hell's Angels. Certainly there are times when these large 1%ers have fought with one another. For example, in 2002, members of the Mongols and the Hell's Angels were involved in a confrontation that left three dead and several wounded. Later in the same year, the Hell's Angels and the Pagans (another large 1%er gang) were involved in a conflict in Long Island regarding turf jurisdiction. This, too, ended in violence and fatalities.

The Hell's Angels

The Hell's Angels were founded in the late 1940s in California. Dressed in black with swastikas on their black jackets, Hell's Angels members garnered international fame as a violent gang when, in 1965, it was commissioned to provide security for a Rolling Stones concert. During the course of the concert, the Angels went into the crowd and created a violent melee (Thompson, 1996). One attendee was killed and several others were injured. In 1970, in a battle with another outlaw gang, the Breed, the Hell's Angels and Breed members suffered massive injuries. Fifty-seven members of both gangs were charged with murder (Thompson, 1999; Lavigne, 1996).

The Hell's Angels, led by Sonny Barger, expanded both in membership and weaponry in the 1950s. Barger was jailed in the 1990s for plotting to bomb a rival's clubhouse (Serwer, 1992). Informants inside the gang state the members are greatly interested in weapons and have large caches that rival those of many small countries (Jeremiah, 2008). Barger has now entered into a new career. He is a published author, writing books on motorcycles, motorcycle etiquette, proper riding techniques, and road trips (Barger, Zimmerman, and Zimmerman, 2001).

Noted as one of the Big Four of the 1%ers, the Hell's Angels are involved in various criminal activities including drug trafficking, assaults, extortion, murder, prostitution, and trafficking in stolen goods. Its membership includes sets around the world that declare a noncriminal mission of setting social events, road trips, and efforts to raise money for charitable causes as well as varied criminal acts (Lindsey, 2005).

There is a proscribed requirement to joining the Hell's Angels. First of all, the candidate must have a driver's license, have a working motorcycle, have no criminal record as a child molester or pedophile, and cannot have applied for employment as a police, correctional, or federal law enforcement officer. After a period of "hanging around," the full membership votes to award the candidate a "full patch" status. In some clubs, the entire membership must approve the new member. In other clubs, the vote required may be a simple majority. Regardless, the patch must be returned after the member leaves the club (Hall, 2005). There are an estimated 3,600 full-time members of the Hell's Angels throughout the world (Dobyns, 2009).

The Bandidos

As with most of the motorcycle gangs of which we have spoken, the Bandidos were founded in the 1960s, actually 1966, in San Leon, Texas. It is a criminal gang, a 1%er. (Winterhalder, 2005).

The Bandidos are headquartered in Texas. The Australian Bandidos are called the Comanchero Motorcycle Club.

The Bandidos were founded by Don Chambers, a former Marine and veteran of the Vietnam War. He is now deceased. After Chambers was charged and found guilty of murder, the presidency was passed on to another member, Ronnie Hodge (Dulaney, 2005). From this beginning over 45 years ago, the Bandidos have built chapters around the world with sets in Europe, Australia, and southeast Asia (Caine, 2009).

This 1%er gang has a long history of criminal activity. For example, in 2004, a man was found fatally stabbed multiple times. The victim was Robert Quiroga, Super Flyweight Champion of the World. A member of the Bandidos was found guilty of the offense (http://www,woai.com/most popular/story.asp?/content-id-d3e0dce-483a-9424-fb66fi3a6260).

The Pagans

The Pagans Motorcycle Club was founded in 1959 in Maryland. The founder was Lou Dobkins, (a biochemist at the National Institute of Health). Originally clad in white denim jackets and riding Triumphs, the gang evolved along the lines of the California stereotype generated by such famous motorcycle clubs as the Outlaws, the Hell's Angels, and the Mongols. After its founding, the Pagans quickly turned into a 1%er gang. Violence and crime became almost a style of life. As far as some of the other clubs are concerned, the Pagans are small in numbers. It may only have as many as 400 members, according to their own homepage.

Motto of the Pagans: "Respect Few, Fear None."

Gang Structure

The typical internal organization of a motorcycle club consists, as depicted in an earlier section of this chapter, of a president, vice president, treasurer, secretary, road captain, and sergeant at arms.

Table 5.2   Influential Biker Movies

Name	Star	Date
The World's Fastest Indian	Anthony Hopkins	2005
Electra Glide in Blue	Robert Blake	2005
Easy Rider	Peter Fonda	1969
Hell's Angels on Wheels	Jack Nicholson	1967
The Wild One	Marlon Brando	1953

Single, large motorcycle gangs are called chapters, and the first chapter established for a motorcycle club is referred to as the "mother" chapter. The president of the mother chapter serves as the president of the entire motor-cycle club, and sets club policy on a variety of issues (Jones, 2001).

One-percenter OMCs (outlaw motorcycle clubs) do not allow women to become full members; women are submissive to the men, treated as property, victimized by forcing them into prostitution or street-level drug trafficking, and are often physically and sexually abused. Any pay women receive is given to their individual men and sometimes to the entire club. Women's roles, as well as their status as objects, make these groups completely male dominated and gender segregated (Adler and Adler, 1994; Barker, 2005).

"Being Full Patched": Being a full member of the motorcycle gang.

The media has been responsible for providing the American public with images, both true but more often false, of the motorcycle clubs and their members. Perhaps one of the earliest influential media portrayals was the movie, *The Wild One*, starring young actor Marlon Brando, originally released in 1953. This movie was quickly followed by others, but it would more than 10 years before the classic, *Easy Rider*, starring Peter Fonda was released. There were others to follow (Table 5.2).

Conclusion

Motorcycle clubs, at least the ones of the Big Four we have spoken of in this chapter, are an American invention. They are also 1%ers. They have moved from social clubs where the male members get together every so often, drinking alcoholic beverages, and exercising an activity of brotherhood, to darker criminal activities of murder, drug smuggling, prostitution, and many other forms of organized crime. They may be the next face of organized crime in this country. What are the characteristics of the gang crimes of the future? Really, only time will tell.

There have been some movements toward the investigation of motor-cycle gangs and its negative influence on the American life and the American dream. The Drug Enforcement Administration (DEA), the Federal Bureau of Investigation (FBI), and other federal agencies have initiated efforts to infiltrate the gangs and have been instrumental in aiding the courts in placing many gang members and leaders in prison. Unfortunately, while they are in prison, they continue their old ways inside the walls with cliques and other gangs inside and outside the institutions. (See Chapter 11 for a more complete discussion of law enforcement and gangs.)

Where does this all lead? This is a good question to which there is no easy answer. We can be thankful, on the one hand, there are the 99%ers who are law-abiding and follow the dictates of society. We believe there needs to be a more uniform and concentrated effort on the part of all law enforcement to face this social problem; local, state, and federal law enforcement agencies need to work together. Then, and only then, can real progress be made. Until then, innocent citizens will continue to be hurt, maimed, and murdered.

Discussion Questions

1. Discuss the basic start of motorcycle gangs in the United States. What happened in the United States to engage such a drastic beginning and kept the gangs ongoing?
2. What are 1%er gangs and how did they get their names?
3. Who are the members of the "Big Four" gangs? Why only these gangs?
4. Discuss the importance of the Harley-Davidson motorcycle as the cycle of choice for the 1%ers.
5. Where is the closest 1%er club in your community? Any police activities? Any special unit involved in the investigations of their crimes?

Suggested Readings

Barker, T. 2007. *Biker gangs and organized crime*. Cincinnati: Anderson Publishing.
Dicks, S. 2002. *Road angels: Women who ride motorcycles*. Los Angeles: Writers Club Press.
Ferrer, A. 1996. *Hear me roar: Women, motorcycles, and the rapture of the road*. New York: Three Rivers Press.
Mullins, S. 2002. *Bikerlady: Living and riding free*. New York: Citadel Press.
Sadgirl. 2010. *The other side of the fence: Love, loyalty, respect, betrayal: A woman in the motorcycle club world*. Denver: Outskirts Press.
Thompson, H. 1965. The motorcycle gangs. *The Nation*, May 17, pp. 1–8.
Veno, A. 2010. *The brotherhoods: Inside the outlaw motorcycle clubs*. Auckland, New Zealand: Allen & Unwin.

The Outlaws Motorcycle Gang

6

> An Outlaw Motorcycle Gang: An organization whose members use their clubs as criminal enterprises.

Motorcycle gangs have been a part of American culture for years. Some may believe that motorcycle gangs only started after World War II. But truly, there were many small and typically law-abiding small clubs prior to this time. Motorcycle gangs truly became a part of the society's counterculture in the late 1940s. The movie industry portrayed a fierce, criminal, cruel, and antisocial group that would later be defined as a 1%er gang, meaning a criminal gang.

Other motorcycle gangs soon followed, and they became household names: the Hell's Angels, the Pagans, and many others, including the Outlaws.

For one of the authors, experience and understanding of the Outlaws comes from personal experience. Growing up in the 1940s and 1950s, I was always aware of the Louisville Outlaws. Maybe it was because of the movie industry and their products, including the classic film *The Wild One*. Those of us who were children at the time learned from our parents and significant others to stay away from these men and their women who wore the Outlaw jacket and rode a Harley-Davidson motorcycle. There was a Hell's Angels gang house not far from my own childhood home. I remember seeing the lineup of bikes parked next to each other on the curb in front of the house. One small girl in my grammar school class had a father in the Louisville Outlaws. He would sometimes pick her up after school on his Harley. One day he rode me home. I held my arms tightly around his waist as my classmate held her arms around my waist.

However, with the house of the gang in my neighborhood, and being a stupid kid, several years later I went up to the front door on a dare of three of my classmates. Just 12 years old, I knocked on the door. A large man, dressed in black with long hair and a beard, opened the door. He asked what I wanted, but I was too scared to reply. He only laughed at me, but invited me inside. I walked inside and was greeted by slurs and curse words including those which attacked my parental background. He invited me into the back room of the shotgun home to the kitchen and offered me a RC Cola. You may ask what was a soda doing in the gang house? I don't know, but I accepted his offer. He asked me questions about myself for the next 15 minutes. He led me back through the house. I left my own bike, a Schwinn with white wall tires, on the front porch. He told me to come back anytime, an invitation which I never honored. I was a hero to my friends who had waited for me a block away. It was a peak experience for me. I did the same thing 60 years later at the Grim Reapers' house in 2010, minus my Schwinn.

After the first episode, I went home and told my parents about my experience. To say the least, they were not pleased and gave me a punishment that caused me some tears. But, I deserved it. My mother asked our parish priest to talk with me, and Father Willett said a special prayer for me when he found out what I had done. I think he prayed to the Sts. Michael and Dymphna, St. Michael being the patron saint of law enforcement and St. Dymphna the patron saint of the mentally ill. I guess there was a message there.

But, maybe from that youthful experience my interest was planted in motorcycle gangs. Even today I want to buy a Harley, or at least a Vespa, something my wife is not willing to accept.

Let us look at a short history of the Outlaws Motorcycle Gang as an example of a 1%er gang.

History of the Outlaws

One of the first American motorcycle clubs was the Yonkers Motorcycle Club founded in 1903. The San Francisco Motorcycle Club was founded the next year. But, after WWII, the real growth began, especially with the 1%er clubs. Many veterans came home from WW II in 1945 abandoning the "American dream" of a wife, a home in the suburbs, and a swarm of children. They elected instead to join a group of other such men who shared their thoughts (Barger, Zimmerman, and Zimmerman, 2001). The Outlaws was one such group.

The modern-day Outlaws were founded in a suburb of Chicago in 1946. By 1950, the sect changed its name to the "Chicago Outlaws," which was later changed to simply "The Outlaws." By the mid 1960s, it changed its name again to "The Outlaw Nation" encompassing other chapters from Milwaukee, Louisville, and several other cities that had recently joined. It truly became a national 1%er organization, interested in drugs, prostitution, murder, and other serious, violent, and deadly crimes. After an early beginning in this fraternal group, crimes against the community became more grave and felonious. Many of the early bikers already had a familiarity with weapons, from handguns to explosives, learned in training and combat in the military in World War II. Their criminal activities quickly captured the attention of law enforcement not only in Chicago, Milwaukee, and Louisville, but across the nation as well (Wethern and Colnett, 2008).

Organization and Definition of Officers

It is certainly not true that all members of the Outlaw Motorcycle Gang have the same and equal status. There are local and national officers that are responsible for various roles and responsibilities.

The organization may appear to many as militarily bureaucratic in nature and scope. This, however, is only somewhat true. The organization closely follows a military model, but there are differences, too. One also must remember, however, that most of the early members of the biker gangs—the Outlaws motorcycle clubs included—were just home from WW II and were veterans. They were used to following orders from the commanding officer and displayed obedience and loyalty to the cause. There were rules and regulations to follow without question. This is true also for the modern-day motorcycle gangs.

If we examine the titles, as shown in Table 6.1, we can easily see the similarities to a true military model. Most police and sheriff's departments also follow the same model, and, so it is with the motorcycle gangs. But, it also includes a governmental model with president, vice president, secretary, and financial officer.

Colors and Patches of Sets and Memberships

As we will see with essentially all motorcycle clubs, individual chapters have unique colors and patches. Clubs or chapters have a full three-piece patch. The top segment of the three-piece patch contains the name of the club or chapter. The middle part of the patch contains the club logo, and the bottom of the three-piece patch contains the location of the chapter. One also will see, if the club is an outlaw club, a 1%er patch on the jacket or vest of the member. Incidentally, the member's patch will always remain the property of the club even if the member leaves the club voluntarily, involuntarily, or dies. Additionally, the patch may be worn only by full-pledged members of the club.

A Day in the Life of an Outlaw

In an effort to get a clearer understanding of what it is like to be a member of the Outlaws, we interviewed "Spike," a member of the Louisville Outlaws Motorcycle Club. Our conversation included questions about the club, himself, and his daily life.

Table 6.1　Officers and Duties of the Outlaw Motorcycle Gang

Name of Office	Duties of the Office
National President	Often the founder of the motorcycle gang. His word is often the rule for the other members.
National Vice Presidentt	Often representatives from other national or regional sets of the outlaw motorcycle gang. Each vice president is in charge of a certain regional area.
National Enforcer	This officer is directly responsible to the national president. He (deliberately a male) will handle discipline matters and retrieve Outlaw materials from members who have voluntarily left the organization.
National Secretary Treasurer	He is responsible for the money matters of the club. He also records minutes of meetings and changes in the club's bylaws.
Chapter President	This person, elected or selected, is responsible for all matters in a local chapter.
Chapter Vice President	Usually selected by the chapter president, he will oversee the matters of the motorcycle club in the absence of the chapter president.
Chapter Secretary/President	Responsible for same matters as the national secretary/treasurer. But his duties are limited to the local chapter.
Chapter Sergeant at Arms	This officer is responsible for maintaining order and discipline at the club's meetings. He is the club's enforcer.
Road Captain	This person has the duty and responsibility of any runs or outings for the club. He will route the roads of travel, arrange for sanitary needs, and food. Oddly, he also is responsible for money during these activities.
Members	These are the rank and file members of the club. They answer allegiance to the president and to abide by the regulations of the club.
Probate or Associate Members	These are prospective members who will have to prove their worthiness to the club. This probationary period may last from one month to one year.
Honorary Members	These are persons who have proved their worthiness by aiding the club in various ways. It can be an attorney who helped them in their criminal cases, or business people who have given money to the club. They are allowed to party with the club, but may not wear patches or colors.

Source:　The Outlaws Web page. www.outlawsmc.com

I first ran into Spike as I was riding in my car along a city street. He pulled up next to me and I spoke to him while we both waited for the red light to turn. We talked more after we both stopped at a second traffic light and then pulled into a gas station. As we were both filling our gas tanks, I told him I was writing a chapter for a book about the Outlaws and would he mind if I asked him a question or two? He said he was busy, but could take out a couple minutes if I would buy him a beer. I did, and we both sat down beside each other, myself wearing a white shirt and a tie with a pair of loafers and khaki pants, and him with long, graying hair pulled up into a pony tail, and the traditional garb of an Outlaw along with colors and patches.

Spike was originally from Portland, Kentucky, a small section of the city in the western part of Louisville. He attended a local Catholic grammar school in the west end of Louisville, and later graduated from a local Catholic high school, also in western Louisville. He enlisted in the army as soon as he graduated and saw several tours of duty in Vietnam. Interestingly enough, he said after he came back home, he missed the friendship of belonging to a brotherhood as well as the sense of danger, and tried to join a local motorcycle club in west Louisville that had a clubhouse about two blocks from his mother's home. After a relatively short time, to regain those powerful and close feelings, he joined a small, local, 1%er motorcycle gang.

Spike said that he finally was approached by the Outlaws because he had several friends who were members, and he immediately left the other gang. It took him several months, he could not remember how many, to become a full-fledged member of the Outlaws, but he finally did.

Spike never married, but he stated he has "probably" had least a dozen children by many women who are affiliates of the set to which he belongs. He said he never is at a loss for female companionship. There are many women who are associated with the motorcycle club, and they are all willing to have sex with the men. His own club has at least a dozen women who serve the men of the club in a variety of ways, not only sexually, but by preparing meals, administering care when appropriate, cleaning the club house, and performing other perfunctory chores.

"Old Ladies:" Motorcycle gang slang for the women who are affiliated with the club and offer services to the male members, including sex and other duties.

He added that his days are never boring. At present, there are no turf battles in the area. The other clubs seem to live in harmony with one another. He said that this is unusual because there are other gangs, such as the Pagans, the Hell's Angels, the Mongols, and others, all present in the community. He pointed out that in September, 2010, the gangs all represented themselves at

Figure 6.1 Dayton, Ohio Outlaws Patch. (From the FBI.)

an annual, local community festival and there was no trouble with any of the members of the clubs. Spike added that almost every night there is drinking, minor drug use (I am not certain he was telling the truth), and sex with the women (the "old ladies") or the "hangers-on" of the club. He also added that there were many activities for the men to become involved in, and they are also involved in "runs."

These runs are offered at various times of the year and the men, some-times with women mounted on the back of their motorcycles, all travel together to various locations. Most of the runs are local where they can leave the clubhouse in the morning and return home by nightfall. However, Spike said the club was driving to Orlando soon for a national meeting near Disney World.

As far as crime is concerned, he said that he had been involved in minor transgressions of the law. He denied any use of illegal drugs, the stealing of drugs, and any personal violent acts directed against others (Figure 6.1). I asked him about the use of women, and he said that the women were always willing and if they wished to no longer be affiliated with the club, it was their choice to leave if they wished. But, when I asked about using the women as prostitutes, he admitted that sometimes the women are escorted to various locales in the community that are "busy locations" for prostitution and the men stay close by to watch out for their safety while they turn a trick. Of course, the money that the women earn belongs to the club.

It appears that not everything Spike stated was true, at least on a national scale. For example, in the past months, there has been a federal investigation into the criminal activities of the Outlaws. An informant, Lyle Beatty, aka "Butchie," became an informant for the FBI. The FBI suc-cessfully recruited him and agreed to pay him $75,000, which included $9,000 for a new motorcycle because his old one was repossessed, as well as not prosecuting him for the possession of a firearm (O'Dell, 2010). The prosecutor, a U.S. attorney, informed the jury that the Outlaws commit murder, assaults, robberies, arson, extortion, and firearms offenses in an attempt largely to gain an advantage over their rivals, the Hell's Angels. The case is still under federal investigation at the time of this writing (O'Dell, 2010).

Selected Patch Abbreviations

.F.F.	This is used by Clubs to say, "[Club Name] Forever, Forever [Club Name]."
1%er	Used by any biker who believes he is part of the "outlaw biker community."
9 or 9er	The wearer of the number is of American Indian descent.
Ace of Spades	The wearer will defend himself and the club to his last breath.
DILLIGAF	Means "Does It Look Like I Give a F----."
G.F.O.D.	"God Forgives, Outlaws Don't."
I.T.C.O.B.	Worn by an outlaw biker who killed on behalf of the club. "I Took Care of Business."
Skull and Crossbones	The wearer has physically fought and may have even murdered for the gang.
Wings	Worn to indicate different awards the biker has achieved.
MC or MCC	Motorcycle club
13	May stand for marijuana, or the wearer is the judge and jury (12 + 1 = 13).
Bad Influence	The wearer is a "bad man."

Criminal Behaviors

Early on, the behaviors of the Outlaws Motorcycle Gang were focused typically on a life of crime. True, many joined for a sense of belonging, danger, and collegiality. Remember, many had just returned home from war, and they simply were not satisfied with a sedate, suburban, all-American type of family and existence. They wanted the joys, rewards, and dangers they had experienced in the military they had just left.

What kinds of crime did the early motorcycle gang member commit? In the early days and even today, prostitution places into the club's financial coffers more money than any other criminal endeavor. Illegal drug activity is a close second. Even today, these two criminal activities prove very profitable to the clubs. How profitable? No one knows for certain, and if a figure is offered, it is at best only an educated guess (Figure 6.2).

Randy Michael Yager

DESCRIPTION

Date of Birth:	08-07-56 (has used 08-17-56)	**Hair:**	Dark Brown
Place of Birth:	Indiana	**Eyes:**	Hazel
Height:	5'11"	**Complexion:**	Fair
Weight:	235lbs.	**Sex:**	Male
Build:	Medium	**Race:**	White (appears Hispanic)
Occupation(s):	Owns Car Dealership	**Nationality:**	U.S. Citizen
Scars/Marks:	N/A		
Aliases:	"Mad"		

Remarks

Yager is the regional president of the Outlaw Motorcycle Club and is wanted for violation of federal RICO Laws.

CAUTION: Subject is known to carry firearms. Has previous Federal RICO Conviction. Yager is considered armed and dangerous.

Figure 6.2 ATF Most Wanted Poster.

Brotherhood and Collegiality

The Outlaws are well-represented across the United States. In going to the Web site for the state of Florida (www.outlawsmc.com/html), the site states there are 16 local chapters in that state at the time of this writing. The locations are listed in Table 6.2.

As one can see from the information in Table 6.2, it is apparent that the Outlaws motorcycle gang are well-represented across the state, from the

Table 6.2   Florida's Alleged Sites of the Outlaw Motorcycle Gang by Location

Charlotte County	Cross Bayou
Daytona	Jacksonville
The Florida Keys	Miami
Ocala	Orlando
Osceola	Panama City
Pensacola	St. Petersburg
Tampa	Treasure Coast
West Coast	West Palm Beach

Source: The Outlaws' Web Site, verified with the police in each city.

southern part of Florida, the Florida Keys, and north to Jacksonville and west to Panama City.

Outlaws motto: "God forgives, Outlaws don't."

According to David Rivers, of the Dade County (Florida) Sheriff's Office (personal interview, 2010), it is estimated that there are approximately 300 motorcycle gang members in Florida. He stated that their primary activities are criminal, although some do engage in social and philanthropic activities like gathering toys for children at Christmas. However, it was his opinion that this was only a cover-up for their criminal activities and an attempt to gather a more positive social image in their community.

Conclusion

The Outlaws are a remarkable and well-known motorcycle gang that has been in operation for the past half-century. Originally it was started by veterans returning from a violent and vicious world war where fellowship and brotherhood had a direct relationship with personal survival. Looking for a form of this brotherhood after returning to the states, many war-experienced veterans attempted to recapture those feelings of comradeship, those feelings experienced in the military in the time of war.

With time, the Outlaws turned into a 1%er group. Dissatisfied with their experiences in peacetime society and their perceived lack of appreciation by those in a peacetime world, the gang members quickly turned to crimes of many kinds. Prostitution, drugs, homicides, and many other forms of violent crimes were reputedly quite prevalent in their early years. As time passed, the Outlaws have moved to other forms of crimes, such as drug use, drug distribution, and other crimes of nondrug-related nature.

The Outlaws have become a force to be reckoned with, despite the thought of many that the Outlaws are not the threat to society that others 1%er groups are. For example, retired DEA (Drug Enforcement Administration) federal agent Rick Sanders believes that the Bandidos are the most violent and fastest growing group of outlaw motorcycle gangs both in the United States and across the world today. The Bandidos Motorcycle Club is now commonly considered by law enforcement authorities to be the most aggressive, criminal, and dangerous motorcycle group. What about the Outlaws? Some may believe the Outlaws, while still a societal threat, is not the threat it used to be, but nonetheless, is still a viable concern for citizens and law enforcement alike.

Discussion Questions

1. Discuss the differences and similarities of the "average" motorcycle member of the 1%er genre and the other motorcycle gang members.
2. Discuss the roles of females in the motorcycle gangs.
3. Why do you believe the motorcycle gangs moved from social clubs to gangs of crime?
4. Are there motorcycle gangs in your community? Are they involved with one of the Big Four? Where are they located?
5. Are any motorcycle gangs in your area involved with social and charitable causes? Give examples, if any.

The Pagans
Motorcycle Club

7

The Pagans Motorcycle Club is another 1%er club, and also one of the Big Four clubs as defined by the Federal Bureau of Investigation (FBI). The club is allegedly involved in a multitude of crimes including murder, drug offenses, prostitution, and other personal and violent assaults. How different the Pagans are from the Outlaws, Hell's Angels, and the Bandidos remains to be seen, but the similarities seem to be more prevalent than the differences.

The Pagans have a long history of crime and they have spread in popularity and presence in several states as illustrated in Figure 7.1.

In this chapter we will go into some depth regarding the history, pervasiveness, and the crimes of the Pagans Motorcycle Club.

History of the Pagans Motorcycle Club

The history of the Pagans is relatively short as compared to that of many other clubs. From various sources, it has been ascertained that the Pagans club was founded in 1959 by a young biker, Lou Dobkins of Prince George's County, Maryland. Its present headquarters is located in Delaware County, Pennsylvania (Mallory, 2007).

In the grand scheme of things, the Pagans is a rather large club. There are about 400 fully patched members with 44 chapters located in the 11 states mentioned in Figure 7.1. The crimes that are committed by members of the Pagans are many and diverse. Before discussing the criminal involvement of the Pagans, we will first examine the gang's structure and locations in the United States (Table 7.1).

Membership

There are strict membership qualifications for any "qualified" applicants. For example, the man must be at least 18 years of age (National Drug Intelligence Center, 2002). This is a requirement for each set regardless of its location. This and other requirements are set by the governing body of the club, the mother club, or the ruling council. Additionally, the potential member must have a Harley-Davidson with a certain sized engine. In case the member leaves the club, the motorcycle will go to the club. The member also must relinquish any

Figure 7.1 Sets of Pagans Motorcycle Gangs in the U.S.

clothing that has the colors and the patches (Figure 7.2) of the club itself. The prospective member must do whatever a patched member demands, be it criminal or noncriminal.

Why would one wish to become a member of the Pagans? There are several good reasons, at least from the perspective of the member himself. For example, as with other motorcycle gangs, the club yields a sense of belonging with other men with the same interests and "hobbies." There is a lack of judgment about the behaviors among members as long as the rules and regulations of the club itself are followed.

The membership within the motorcycle club provides the member with a sense of power and control. This power and control is directed, obviously, toward others who are more vulnerable, the physically smaller, those who are powerless, and with less protection. The members also join because it may be a way of associating with their peers who may help them, in both legal and illegal ways.

Many members of the Pagans, as well as other clubs, are social loners. Some are married, some divorced, and so on. Some are gainfully employed. Some are unemployed and some do not wish to work, only to hang around the clubhouse, drink, do drugs, have sex with "the old ladies" (those women who are affiliated with the club and offer services to the male members), and live a life of leisure. The sole motorcycle of choice for the Pagans is a Harley-Davidson with engines 900 cc or larger.

Table 7.1 Overview of American Motorcycle Gangs

Motorcycle Club Name	Location	Number of Members	Alleged Criminal Activities	Founded In	Allies with Gangs, Such As …	Rivals with Gangs, Such As …
Vacos	California	300	Drugs Murder Stolen property	1965		Hell's Angels
Free Souls	Oregon	100	Drugs Auto theft Arms dealings	1968		Vacos
Bandidos	Texas	2,500	Drugs Murder Stolen property	1966	Outlaws Mongols	Hell's Angels Sons of Silence
Highwaymen	Michigan	200	Drugs Prostitution Murder Racketeering	1954	Sons of Silence	Outlaws
Warlocks	Pennsylvania	500	Drugs Murder Burglary Kidnapping	1967	Hell's Angels Sons of Silence	
Sons of Silence	Colorado	275	Drugs Murder Prostitution	1966	Highwaymen Warlocks	Bandidos
Outlaws	Illinois	1,700	Bombing Murder Prostitution	1935	Mongols Pagans Bandidos	Hell's Angels Highwaymen

(Continued)

Table 7.1 (Continued) Overview of American Motorcycle Gangs

Motorcycle Club Name	Location	Number of Members	Alleged Criminal Activities	Founded In	Allies with Gangs, Such As ...	Rivals with Gangs, Such As ...
Pagans	Maryland	400	Murder Extortion Arson Prostitution	1959	Bandidos Mongols Outlaws	Hell's Angels The Breed
Mongols	California	600	Illegal firearm sales Murder Drugs	1969		Hell's Angels Free Souls
Hell's Angels	California	3,600	Racketeering Murder Drugs	1948	Aryan Brotherhood	Pagans Bandidos
Iron Horsemen	Ohio	Unknown	Drugs Prostitution	1965	Hell's Angels Sons of Silence	Outlaws

Source: Barker, 2005.

Figure 7.2 Pagans Motorcycle Club's insignia. (From the FBI.)

Table 7.2 Women and the Pagans

Club Name for a Woman	Definition
Old Lady	Wives or steady girlfriends of the club members
Honeys	Women who can be given or sold to another set
Train Honeys	Same as honeys

As is true with most outlaw motorcycle clubs, women have no rights and are not to be trusted with any information open only to the male members. The "old ladies" are the wives or steady girlfriends of the chapter members (Table 7.2). They are allowed to wear special patches that designate them as restricted property of a particular member. In some clubs, members may be able to have more than one "old lady," and the "old ladies" may be shared with other male members.

Criminal Activities

The Pagans Motorcycle Club is allegedly involved in a variety of crimes. As alluded to earlier, these crimes are numerous and wide-ranging. For example, as mentioned, murder, drug crimes, drugs, crimes perpetrated against other gangs, (such as the Outlaws, their principle rival), crimes for organized crime, arson, car theft, motorcycle theft, and weapons trafficking are prevalent. These are all ongoing criminal activities and it appears there is no downturn in frequency regarding the crimes committed by the club (Table 7.3).

In Charleston, West Virginia, in 2009, the federal government was able to charge more than 50 members of the Pagans on charges of kidnapping, robbery, extortion, conspiracy to commit murder, and others crimes in the club's effort to be the preeminent motorcycle gang in the Eastern region of the United States. One of the defendants was the national vice president of the Pagans Motorcycle Club, Floyd "Jesse" Moore. Moore was accused of hiring a prison guard to get to a prison inmate to kill him because Moore believed he was a government informant. Moore also was accused of ordering two Pagans to beat up a member of a minor motorcycle club. He pled guilty to federal RICO charges and received a sentence of four years, nine months in prison (Associated Press, 2011).

Table 7.3   Crimes by and against the Pagans Motorcycle Clubs

Date	Location	Description
February 2002	Long Island	In a fight with the Outlaws at a gathering, the Pagans and the Outlaws engaged in a fight. Ten people were wounded and one Pagan died.
March 2002	Philadelphia	The Pagans' tattoo parlor was demolished allegedly by the Outlaws.
July 2005	Philadelphia	The Pagans allegedly shot and killed the Outlaws' vice president on the local expressway.
September 2010	Rocky Point, New York	Nineteen members of the Pagans were arrested for allegedly conspiring to murder members of the Hell's Angels.
May 2007	Maryland	A Pagans member, Jay Wagner, was arrested for allegedly planting a bomb.
March 2008	Maryland	Wagner pleaded guilty to possession of a firearm.
August 2008	Maryland	Wagner sentenced to 30 months in prison and 3 years on supervised release.
2009	Various states, arraigned in West Virginia	Fifty-five members of the motorcycle club from West Virginia, Kentucky, Virginia, Pennsylvania, New York, New Jersey, Delaware, and Florida.
2010	Long Island, New Jersey, Delaware	Nineteen members of the Pagans after an undercover federal agents discovered a plot to kill Hell's Angels bikers.

Source: Associated Press, New York Daily News, "National Pagans Motorcycle Club members indicted in biker plot," October 7, 2010; Marzulli, J. 2010. "Pagans biker gang plotted to kill Hell's Angels with grenade attacks, says Feds." *New York Daily News*.

The Pagans, like many other outlaw motorcycle gangs, have a great deal of interest in drugs as a manner of making money for the gang's uses. Table 7.4 contains information concerning the most common drugs used by the Pagans as well as other outlaw motorcycle clubs.

Law enforcement on the local, state, and federal levels are very active in the investigation of and aiding in the prosecution of the Pagans. For example, in Baltimore, Maryland, in 2008, the state police and the Bureau of Alcohol, Tobacco, and Firearms (ATF) arrested Jay Carl Wagner, age 66, on charges of being a felon in possession of a firearm. Wagner faces a 10-year sentence on that charge. However, at the time of this writing, all charges and sentences have not been resolved (Miller, 2010). Among Pagans who have been identified as allegedly involved in serious criminal activity is their national president and national vice president.

In 2010, 17 alleged Pagan members and associates were indicted again for a large number of federal crime: racketeering, drugs, witness tampering, attempted murder, firearm violations, and other charges. In this case, the Pagan Motorcycle Club's main target was the Hell's Angels. The federal agents learned in their investigation that members of the Pagan Motorcycle Club were planning to use grenades in their attack on the Hell's Angels Motorcycle Club. The president of one chapter of the Pagan Motorcycle Club had allegedly instructed some of the members of his club to kill or be prepared to die or go to prison if they did not follow his directions.

Table 7.4 Drugs Often Allegedly Used by the Pagans

Name of Drug	Description
Cocaine	It appears that most outlaw clubs receive their supplies of cocaine from large markets such as California, Chicago, and Detroit. Many times the drug is purchased from street gangs, such as MS-13, the Vice Lords, and the Crips.
Heroin	Heroin is often sold by street gangs to clubs and club members and many times by the Hispanic and African-American street gangs.
Methamphetamine	There are many cases of clubs and gangs that manufacture their own drugs, which are made in homemade meth labs. Most of these labs are toxic and capable of producing only a few ounces at a time.
Club Drugs	Many clubs are involved in so-called club drugs including MDMA (ecstasy), Ketamine, GHB, GBL Rohypnol, LSD, PCP, and psilocybin mushrooms. These same drugs is also involved with young nonclub and nongang members are raves and nightclubs across the country.
Marijuana	With most clubs, it appears that marijuana is the common and popular drug of choice. It is easily available to club members and noncriminal community members.
Other Drugs	Diverted controlled substances, such as Oxycodone, Ritalin, methadone, and Nubain.

In Pittsburgh, six Pagans were charged with racketeering and firearms violations. The six men, ranging in age from 26 to 57, testified in court that they were instructed to commit crimes as a part of their initiation into the motorcycle club (Peirce, 2009). In court, the witnesses testified that they were beaten by another member because they did not do as he told them to do. Their beatings included the use of baseball bats, and punishments included making them do chores around the clubhouse. The member who allegedly carried out these beatings, Raymond Overly, vanished in November 2009, and is on the Most Wanted List of the U.S. Department of Justice (Figure 7.3) (Peirce, 2009).

U.S. Department of Justice
United States Marshals Service

Name: Raymond Edward OVERLY
Gang Affiliation: Pagans

Description:
Sex: Male
Race: White
Date of Birth: 03/20/1971
Place of Birth: Pennsylvania
Height: 5'09"
Weight: 170
Eyes: Brown
Hair: Brown

Wanted For: Felony Drug Violations (14 counts)
Date of Warrant: 06/02/2009
Issuing Agency: Pennsylvania State Police

CAUTION – ARMED AND DANGEROUS

On June 02, 2009 a warrant for the arrest of Raymond OVERLY was issued by the Westmoreland County Court of Common Pleas for 14 counts of Felony Drug Violations, 14 counts of Criminal Conspiracy – Controlled Substance, Theft by Unlawful Taking, and Corrupt Organizations. The warrants stem from a 2006 Pennsylvania State Police criminal investigation. Raymond OVERLY is additionally wanted for Failure to Appear for an Aggravated Assault charge.

Raymond OVERLY remains at large and is considered armed and dangerous. OVERLY has an extensive violent criminal history and is an active member of the Pagan's outlaw motorcycle gang.

NOTICE: Before arrest, verify warrant through the National Crime Information Center (NCIC). If subject is arrested or whereabouts known, contact the nearest U.S. Marshals Service office or call the U.S. Marshals Service Communications center at **1-800-336-0102.**

For more information, see the GangTECC or U.S. Marshals website:
www.usdoj.gov/criminal/gangtecc
www.usmarshals.gov

Figure 7.3 Most Wanted Poster by the U.S. Marshals of Ray Overly, a member of the Pagans Motorcycle Club.

Patches and Colors

Like other motorcycle clubs, the Pagans have certain colors and patches that easily identify the wearer as a Pagan. The Pagans' colors are red, blue, and white. However, the most important and, perhaps, the most visible is the patch of the member. The Pagans MC patch depicts the Norse fire giant Surtr (Mallory, 2007, pp. 157–160), sitting on the sun, wielding a sword, plus the word *Pagan's* [sic] in red, white, and blue. There is no bottom rocker number denoting the club's full patch. It is believed the club declines to follow this 1%er tradition because they do not want law enforcement to know to which chapters individual Pagans belong. There is another thought that the Pagans are declining in numbers because of the wars that have developed between the Pagans and the Outlaws Motorcycle Club.

Members wear blue denim vests called cuts or cutoffs with club patches, known as colors, on the front and back, and symbols of the Pagans also include a black number 13 on the back of their colors. Patches are as different as the motorcycle clubs (Table 7.5). They each have different colors and patches and within the patch are abbreviations that are difficult to decipher unless one is familiar with the club or outlaw motorcycle gangs generally (Figure 7.4).

Chapters and Subsets

According to the FBI, the Pagans Motorcycle Gang has at least 400 members in 11 different states. The National Drug Intelligence Center (2002) reports that the Pagans Motorcycle Club is the nation's largest outlaw criminal

Table 7.5   Selected Patch Abbreviations

Abbreviation	Meaning
1%er	Biker who considers himself a part of the "Outlaw" biker community
4	Pagan motto: "Live and Die"
5	Nazi SS motto
9er	Biker of Native American descent
Ace of Spades	The member will defend the club to the member's death or the other person's death
G.F.O.D.	"God forgives, Outlaws don't"
MC/MCC	Motorcycle Club
Men of Mayhem	This is worn by members who have committed crimes of violence against others for the club
Skull and Crossbones	The members have been involved in a physical fight that may have resulted in a death
Wings	Indicates the person has done special favors for the club

Figure 7.4 Patch of the Pagans Motorcycle Club.

organization in the United States. Additionally, we can see that the Pagans Motorcycle Club is an international gang dedicated to crime, including acts of violence, such as murder and rape. And, the club is also a social club for its members, granting them a sense of belonging and solidarity. It also functions—like many gangs of all varieties—to give them a home where they can interact with others with similar personal traits and characteristics. In this way, as with almost all gangs of all varieties, the gang alleviates experiences of aloneness, boredom, and loneliness.

Conclusion

The Pagans have a long history of both property and personal crimes as well as an increased use of drugs and of the selling of illegal drugs. There are no indications that this form of illegal activity is ceasing or decreasing. If this is true, then the Pagans continue to be a source of criminal activity that is worthy of the time, energy, and manpower dedicated to the removal of the very real criminal and social problem. The removal of such gangs in any community would result in the lowering of crime rates and make the community a safer and better place to live.

Discussion Questions

1. The Pagans are located primarily in one section of the United States. Why is that? Give some reasons.
2. The Pagans are allegedly involved in the manufacturing and selling of meth as a quick manner of making money. Why would this be so?
3. Why does the Pagans Motorcycle Club, a 1%er group, insist on Harley-Davidson motorcycles?
4. How much of a problem is the Pagans Motorcycle Club in your area?
5. Where are the local 1%er motorcycle groups located in your community? How visible are they?

Suggested Readings

Bates, A. 2010. *The Pagans*. Charleston, SC: BiblioBazaar.

Surhone, L., M. Timpledon, and S. Marseken. 2010. *Pagans Motorcycle Club: Outlaw Motorcycle Club, Prince George's County, Maryland, Triump Engineering Co., LTD, Hell's Angels*. Port Louis, Mauritius: Betascript Publishing.

The Bandidos Motorcycle Club

8

Introduction

The third of the "Big Four" motorcycle clubs is the Bandidos Motorcycle Club. The Bandidos is a 1%er group and is heavily involved in crimes, including illegal drugs and crimes of violence. They are not unlike the Hell's Angels, the Outlaws, and the Pagans motorcycle gangs in this respect. However, the U.S. Drug Enforcement Administration (DEA) believes that this is the most violent motorcycle club and one of the most rapidly rising in members of all the Big Four clubs (Sanders, 2010).

A Short History of the Bandidos Motorcycle Club

Bandido's Credo

A 1%er is the 1% of a hundred of us who have given up on society. And the politicians' one-way law. This is why we look repulsive. We're saying we don't want to be like you or look like you. So, stay out of our face.

The Bandidos Motorcycle Club was founded like many other motorcycle clubs in the 1960s. With the unrest in American society, the war in Vietnam, and the unrest among those returning from active duty in the various military units of the U.S. government, the returning veterans were often suffering from posttraumatic stress. A lack of personal bonding with other men like they had developed with members of the military while in the service, their own unrest as well as a sense of a lack of appreciation by the average citizens for what they had done in the war itself, caused many to turn to others who shared many of their own thoughts and values. A dissatisfaction and lack of respect for the U.S government permeated many of the motorcyclists' minds and mentalities. They sought an outlet for their feelings and their needs, and the motorcycle clubs seemed to be the best social club to meet their needs.

Many of the early days of the clubs were social in nature. Perhaps trying to reestablish that sense of brotherhood and belonging, the early clubs fulfilled that need, but did little to satisfy the urges of violence and the use of weapons that they were all taught in a responsible fashion in war. But now, psychologically needing the thrill and excitement of the perpetration of personal violence, clubs such as the Outlaws, Hell's Angels, the Pagans, and the Bandidos Motorcycle Club turned from law-abiding social clubs to criminal gangs.

The Bandidos Motorcycle Club was founded in 1966 in San Leon, Texas, by a former U.S. marine, Don Chambers, who became the national leader of the Bandidos and was later sentenced to life in prison for murder. The presidency was passed from Chambers after he was sent to prison with another Bandido member, Ronnie Hodge (Delaney, 2005). Despite the problems with the law and prison sentences of its members, the Bandido chapters continue to grow and expand. Their growth not only was evident in the growing chapters within the confines of North America, but in many other parts of the world, as shown in Table 8.1.

Criminal History of the Bandidos Motorcycle Club

As mentioned above, the Bandidos Motorcycle Club is a criminal gang or club. It is a 1%er group with a history of criminal activities going back to the early years of their founding. Of course, the members of the Big Four are continually involved in crimes, and the traits and character of the crimes have changed over the years to a newer character of terrorism that has enlarged its circle of criminal activity and violence to people outside the gang (Barker and Human, 2009).

From the information in Table 8.2, it is seen that most of the sets or chapters of the Bandidos Motorcycle Clubs are located in Texas, Washington, and other western states, such as South Dakota, Montana, Colorado, and southern states such as Louisiana, with some Midwestern states also included. The information for this table was obtained from the official Web site of the Bandidos and we can only report on what is listed and have no way of knowing its accuracy.

From the initial beginnings of the Bandidos Motorcycle Club, there has been evidence of a move away from the organization emphasizing social activities and brotherhood toward being a fully developed criminal organization intent on committing various crimes, including:

- Conspiracy to murder
- Conspiracy to distribute marijuana

Table 8.1   Nations with Bandidos Chapters

Bandidos Chapters around the World	
Australia	Belgium
Canada	Costa Rica
Denmark	France
Germany	Italy
Luxemburg	Malaysia
Norway	Singapore
Sweden	Thailand
Finland	United States

- Conspiracy and distribution of methamphetamine
- Drug smuggling
- Murder
- Rape
- Theft of cars, motorcycles, other forms of property
- Firearm violations
- Prostitution

In the summer of 2004, former Super Flyweight Boxing Champion Robert Quiroga was found dead next to his car as a result of multiple stab

Table 8.2   Locations of Bandidos Chapters in the United States

Abilene, TX	El Paso, TX	Oahu, HI
Alamogordo, NM	Elko, NV	Panhandle North, TX
Albuquerque North, NM	Ellis Co., TX	Plainview, TX
Albuquerque South, NM	Everett, WA	Pueblo, CO
Albuquerque West, NM	Forth Worth, TX	Rapid City, SD
Albuquerque, NM	Gallup, NM	Roswell, NM
Amarillo, TX	Galveston, TX	Ruidoso, NM
Atchison, KS	Gillette, WY	San Antonio Centro, TX
Auburn, WA	Grand Junction, CO	San Antonio NW, TX
Austin, TX	Heart of Texas, TX	San Antonio SW, TX
Baton Rouge, LA	Hill Country, TX	San Antonio, TX
Baytown, TX	Houston West, TX	San Leon, TX
Beaumont, TX	Houston, TX	Seattle North, WA
Bellingham, WA	Huntsville, AL	Seattle South, WA
Billings, MT	Jackson, MS	Seattle, WA
Biloxi, MS	Jefferson Co., TX	Shreveport, LA
Birmingham, AL	Kerville, TX	Skagit, WA
Black Hills, SD	Lafayette, LA	Spokane, WA
Boot Hill, NE	Laredo, TX	Tacoma Centro, WA
Bremerton, WA	Las Cruces, NM	Tacoma, WA
Carlsbad, NM	Las Vegas, NV	Tooele, UT
Centro, NM	Lawton, OK	Tres Rios, WA
Chelan County, WA	Little Rock, AR	Tri-Cities, WA
Cloverleaf, TX	Longview, TX	Truth or Consequences, NM
Corpus Christi, TX	Lubbock, TX	Tulsa North, OK
Dallas, TX	Missoula, MT	Tulsa, OK
DeClod, ID	Mobile, AL	Waco, TX
Denton, TX	Montgomery, AL	Whatcom County, WA
Denver, CO	Mount Hull, WA	Yakima, WA
East River, SD	New Orleans, LA	Yakima, WA
El Centro Denver, CO	North County, WA	

Source: Bandidos Motorcycle Club Web site. www.bandidosmc.dk.

wounds. After three years of investigation by the local authorities, it resulted in the arrest of Ricky Merla, a former member of the Bandidos (Figure 8.1). The outlaw biker was found guilty in Quiroga's murder and was sentenced in 2007 to 40 years in prison.

There have been other Bandidos who also have been allegedly involved in serious crimes of violence, including national presidents as well as chapter presidents. Don Chambers, now deceased, served time in prison for criminal activities committed by the Bandidos Motorcycle Gang, including two murders. James Lang, Craig Johnston, Glenn Merritt (sentenced to four years in prison), and George Wegers (sentenced to 20 months in prison and three years probation) are all former national presidents or chapter presidents who served time in prison for criminal acts.

Murder is not the only crime that can be attributed to the Bandidos Motorcycle Club. However, murder is something from which the Bandidos do not seem to shy away. Sanders (2010) reported that in his time as a federal agent, it was the government's thought that the Bandidos was responsible for more than 700 murders. The methods of killings included burnings, shootings, hangings, dying in explosions, beheadings, poisonings, and drowning. However, the reader must be warned. The numbers have been difficult, if not impossible, to prove.

Bandidos Motorcycle Club Slogans

We are the people your parents warned you about.
If you can't be well-liked, be well-hated.
Cut one ... we all BLEED.

Perhaps the most famous criminal activity the Bandidos Motorcycle Club was involved in occurred in Toronto, Canada, in 2006. Apparently, because of an

Figure 8.1 Patch of Bandidos Motorcycle Club. (Author's files.)

impending schism involved in the motorcycle gangs and subservient chapters, one leader of the Bandidos Motorcycle Club ordered the deaths of several members of the Bandidos and hangers-on. Eight members of the Bandidos were found dead in several cars in a barren and remote area in southwestern Toronto. The crime scene was described as gruesome and horrific by investigators, with the victims often shot in the head and their faces smeared with their own blood.

Six members of the Bandidos were arrested and charged with the murders. Bandidos member Wayne Kellestine, called a psychopath and sadistic killer by the prosecution, was said to be the head of the attack squad (Edwards, 2009).

In another case, 26 Bandidos were indicted in Seattle, Washington, by a federal grand jury on charges of federal racketeering and other violent crimes. The grand jury investigation found the Bandidos were involved in numerous federal crimes in three states: Washington, Montana, and South Dakota. In a raid of the club's facilities, the federal agents found drugs, stolen motorcycles, firearms, money, and marijuana plants. Included in the indictment was the national president of the Bandidos Motorcycle Club, George Wegers (Shukovsky, 2006).

Brotherhood

> I don't believe that you can explain in words what Brotherhood means in our world.
> If you got it, the right ones will know.
> It doesn't come when you buy a Harley,
> It is not part of the warranty
> Nor the leathers you wear.
> It does not come when your break
> In mileage comes around,
> Nor when you get your first
> Service appointment.
> It comes with
> Love, Loyalty, and Respect
> To those who would stand by your side
> In good times and in bad. It comes when
> Your brothers accept that you have what
> It takes to be respected, trusted, and
> Faithful to the end. If it never comes,
> You weren't meant to be a part of it.
> If it does, be proud and don't f#@* it up.

Despite the tremendous efforts of the federal government, as well as local and state law enforcement agencies, the Bandidos Motorcycle Club is expanding across the country and several foreign countries. Their crimes continue and the exact extent of the crimes of various kinds, traits, and seriousness, while unknown regarding many specifics and details, pose a threat not only to their own members but to the general public as well.

Conclusion

From the materials presented in this chapter, we have seen the Bandidos Motorcycle Club as one of the fastest growing 1%er gangs in the United States.

It has chapters in many foreign countries as well and continues to grow at an alarming rate. Starting from humble beginnings, the Bandidos have grown into a formidable legal concern and social problem for law enforcement and society at large. Dealing in drugs, committing fatal acts of violence, and many other acts of predation and crime, it truly may be that the Bandidos are a major force and viable concern for law enforcement agencies at the local, state, and federal levels.

A major effort must be undertaken to gather meaningful intelligence to understand the mind and mentality of the outlaw biker ilk, the manners in which they commit their crimes, and the total understanding, as much as possible, of the structure, officers, and support personnel of the chapters themselves.

Then, and only then, can any successful penetration and eradication of such gangs be possible. This should be our goal, our purpose. We also believe that perhaps by reducing or even eradicating this one form of gang criminal enterprise, it may have some negative impact on future motorcycle gangs as well as street gangs and prison gangs. We believe there is synergism involved within these three groups. What affects one group may have an impact on the other two groups. Anyhow, we hope so.

Discussion Questions

1. Why do you believe that law enforcement considers the Bandidos as one of the most violent clubs and one of the most violent motorcycle groups in the United States today?
2. In your own estimation after reading the chapters on motorcycle gangs, what might be some of the causes for the Bandidos to turn to a life and lifestyle of crime?
3. Discuss the Bandidos' colors and icons in their patch.
4. According to the chart in this chapter, most of the clubs of the Bandidos are located in the western part of the United States. Why would that be?
5. What is the future of the Bandidos Motorcycle Club? Is it to grow and survive, or die out as a viable 1%er gang?

The Hell's Angels 9

Introduction

The Hell's Angels Motorcycle Club is an international motorcycle club and probably one of America's most well-known motorcycle clubs. The U.S. Department of Justice states that the Hell's Angels Motorcycle Club is one of the Big Four outlaw gangs in the United States (National Drug Intelligence Center, 2002). It has been an outlaw presence for the past 60 years, and there is no indication that membership or population, as well as involvement in crime, is in any way diminishing. Its criminal activities are typically centered around drug trafficking plus a plethora of other crimes, which we will discuss in this chapter.

Originally founded in 1948 by Otto Friedli in Fontana, California, the club quickly established its motto: "When we do it right, nobody remembers. When we do wrong, nobody forgets." True, the Federal Bureau of Investigation (FBI), Drug Enforcement Administration (DEA), and Bureau of Alcohol, Tobacco, Firearms, and Explosives (ATF) have all classified the Hell's Angels Motorcycle Club as a criminal gang despite the protests of the members themselves, who insist they are only a social club and not at all interested in committing acts of violence or crimes. However, social scientists have used law enforcement activities and investigations to show that this is not the truth. The Hell's Angels Motorcycle Club does sponsor charity events and other types of similar events, perhaps as a way of sending a prosocial message to the community, but they are widely involved in a vast variety of violent crimes and drug crimes.

To provide a deeper understanding of the Hell's Angels, this chapter begins with a short history of the Hell's Angels Motorcycle Club. The chapter then moves to the specifics of membership. We also present the different patches and colors of the Hell's Angels as well as a presentation of the different charters that the Hell's Angels offer. Finally, the crime and criminal behavior of the Hell's Angels is discussed.

A Short History of the Hell's Angels Motorcycle Club

Shortly after the veterans were discharged and sent back home after WWII, they found themselves separated from the close male relational ties that they had formed in combat. Looking for that same or similar sense of companionship, the young male veterans often chose the motorcycle club as a way of trying to reconnect with that same sense of comradeship they had enjoyed in the military. In seeking this companionship, they experienced a sense of risk, an easily identified enemy, and the permission and "right" to wreak havoc upon those who are in competition or opposed to the gang's ideologies and goals. Sometimes the companionship may result in death.

Some believe that the name of the Hell's Angels Motorcycle Club comes from the United States fighter planes operational in WWI and WWII. The members have gained some semblance of notoriety in America's society (Figure 9.1). In 1969, the Hell's Angels Motorcycle Club was hired to provide security for a Mick Jagger and the Rolling Stones concert. During the concert, a large melee broke out, perhaps started by the Hell's Angels going into the crowd and creating a violent altercation with the crowd. One attendee was killed and many others were injured. Another time, the Hell's Angels members were in a battle with another 1%er group, the Breed, and 57 members of the Hell's Angels Motorcycle Club were charged with murder (Lavigne, 1996; Thompson, 1999).

The Hell's Angels are known for their violence, but they also perform community service. The members are involved in a number of social events and road trips for charitable causes (Lindsey, 2005). In Louisville, Kentucky, every spring, several motorcycle clubs make a short trip in the western part of the city for various charitable causes. Strictly patrolled by the local police, these annuals road trips have been without any serious incident.

Sonny Barger founded the Oakland, California, chapter of the Hell's Angels in 1957. In his book, *Hell's Angel: The Life and Times of Sonny Barger*

Figure 9.1 The Hell's Angels from various locations as illustrated by the third box on the back of their jackets. (From the FBI.)

and the Hell's Angels Motorcycle Club, Barger, along with Keith Zimmerman and Kent Zimmerman (2001), provide the reader with a look at the inside operation of this outlaw motorcycle group. He shares with the reader a look at fights, crimes, and battles with the federal government in the latter's effort to eliminate the Hell's Angels Motorcycle Club. This effort has met with some success, but it has not been totally accepted. In other words, the Hell's Angels Motorcycle Club is still in operation and is considered a major force in drug trafficking.

Another former Hell's Angel, George Wethern, wrote of his times as a member of the Hell's Angels Motorcycle Club. Acting as an informant for the U.S. government, he is presently living under the Witness Protection Program. In his book, the former Angel wrote of his involvement in the gang itself, his involvement with drugs and crime, and the money involved in the illegal drug industry (Wethren and Colnett, 2008).

To illustrate the differences between the Hell's Angels Motorcycle Club in the United States and the same club chapters in Canada, Langton (2010) speaks of the need for the help and aid of the Hell's Angels Motorcycle Club. The Hell's Angels are important in their negotiation tactics and their ability to resolve issues. The manner in which the American chapters have helped resolve the various discords and disputes between other motorcycle gangs (Caine, 2009) often involve personal violence.

However, there are other dangers to being a member of the Hell's Angels. In 2008, the president of the San Francisco chapters of the club was shot and killed in the Mission District of this city. The witnesses stated that Mark "Papa" Guardado was shot after an altercation between him and an unknown killer, who fled the scene on his motorcycle. Van Derbeken (2008) discovered that it was not known if the killing had anything to do with a rival motorcycle gang warfare, but the Mongols are considered to be prime suspects.

Membership Requirements

As with other motorcycle clubs, membership requirements are needed. For example, and this may appear to be simple, the prospective joiner must have a valid driver's license. The prospective member also must have a functional motorcycle, which will usually go to the motorcycle club if the new member decides to get out without the permission of the club itself. The new member also must not have a criminal record at the time of application, not be a pedophile or sex offender, and must not have had a previous application as a police officer, a federal law enforcement officer, or a correctional officer.

The initial stage to become a full-fledged member of the Hell's Angels Motorcycle Club is called a "hanger around." This person is at the lowest rung of the membership ladder. He is at the beck and call of a member of the club, and he is expected to do anything that the member asks, from committing a crime (including murder) to giving his wife or girlfriend to one of the members for sexual purposes. By doing what the club members ask (or demand), the hanger around proves his allegiance and fidelity to the club. Then, and only then, can the person move on to the next step, the "associate" level (Hall, 2005).

The associate has the responsibility of performing more difficult tasks, having a greater role, and carrying increased responsibilities of the club itself. Such activities will include crimes of violence, predating against other rival gangs, including murder, and other activities that the club and members demand.

After a successful time of "probation" with the club, the member is voted upon by the full-fledged members of the set. Some sets will demand that everyone approve the new candidate. Other sets may insist only on a majority vote of the membership. Nonetheless, it is important to understand that the members themselves control the initiation and admission of all members to the club.

The members are supposed to investigate each new member to prevent undercover law enforcement personnel from getting into the club. This does not guarantee that there aren't any undercover law enforcement agents breaking into the "sacred circle" of membership. We have seen this happen often, with not only the Hell's Angels Motorcycle Club, but with other 1%er groups as well. Despite the careful screening of new members, the federal government has been successful in infiltrating its ranks with agents working undercover. For example, Agent David Atwell rose through the ranks of the Hell's Angels to become the director of security. He was eventually responsible for the arrest and prosecution of several members of the Hell's Angels in Toronto. Included in the arrests were: John "Winner" Neal, vice presidents Larry Pooler and Douglas Miles, Mehrdad "Juicy" Bahman, and Lorne Campbell. They face various conspiracy charges associated with trafficking in cocaine, ecstasy, and guns from 2005 through 2007. All have pleaded not guilty at the time of this writing (Pazzano, 2010).

To summarize, to become a "full member," the "prospect" must be voted upon by the full club members. Once the member is accepted as a full member of the Hell's Angels Motorcycle Club and, after a period of "hanging out" with other club members, the applicant may be accepted as a full member. Then, and only then, can the new member receive his "patch." As stated above, the candidate's admission may be blocked by a single vote, or some other clubs may only demand a simple majority. However, again, if the fully patched member leaves the motorcycle club, he must return his patch (Hall, 2005), and, usually, the ex-members' motorcycle also may be confiscated by the club.

According to Dobyns (2009), there are more than 3,500 fully patched members of the Hell's Angels. This number is likely to grow, according to Dobyns.

Patches and Colors of the Hell's Angels Motorcycle Club

The colored patch of the Hell's Angels is composed of red and white. It has a "skull head" emblem on the patch with the number "81" somewhere on or near the patch. The number 8 represents the letter "h" and the number 1 represents the letter "a," thus Hell's Angels Motorcycle Club. There is also the small patch of 1%er, a criminal gang insignia. The 1%er is written in red on a white background.

Hell's Angels Motorcycle Club Charters

There are chapters or charters of the Hell's Angels Motorcycle Club in almost every state in America. In talking, however, with "Master Tom" of the Hell's Angels Motorcycle Club in Kentucky, he said there were chapters in *every* state.

The Hell's Angels Motorcycle Club's Web page lists a variety of foreign countries as places of charters (www.hells-angels.com/?ha=charters):

Canada	Switzerland	Chile
Brazil	Austria	Croatia
Argentina	England	Luxembourg
Australia	Wales	Northern Ireland
South Africa	Finland	Hungary
New Zealand	Norway	Turkey
Spain	Sweden	Poland
France	Denmark	Liechtenstein
Belgium	Greece	Iceland
Holland	Russia	Ireland
Germany	Bohemia	
Italy	Portugal	

Figure 9.2 shows the patch from the Hell's Angels Motorcycle Club located in Australia. The top has the name of the motorcycle club, the middle illustrates the icon of that particular club, and the lower part tells the viewer the location of this particular club. The patch illustrates the widespread membership of this motorcycle club. The above list contains various foreign countries that have Hell's Angels Motorcycle Clubs.

Figure 9.2 Vest and patch of the Hell's Angels Motorcycle Club in Australia. Note the icon. (From the *FBI Law Enforcement Bulletin*.)

Crime, Criminals, and the Hell's Angels Motorcycle Club

We can see that the Hell's Angels Motorcycle Club is an international entity. As a federal agent said to us, the Hell's Angels are spread across the world and are probably the world's largest 1%er group or gang (Sanders, 2010, personal interview). But the Hell's Angels rejects the term "gang." They purport to be a social group and not a gang at all, despite the many times the Hell's Angels members have been involved in crimes and the number who are in prison for various crimes:

- Greg Domey, age 81, currently in a federal prison
- Steven Yee, Ohio Correctional Institution in Levettsburg, Hell's Angels Motorcycle Club, Cleveland, Ohio
- John Bonds, Minersville, Pennsylvania Corrections, Charter—Hell's Angels Motorcycle Club, Cleveland, Ohio
- Chris Wilson, Wisconsin Correctional Facility, Charter—Hell's Angels Motorcycle Club, Las Vegas, Nevada
- Johnny Bart, Ohio Correctional Facility, Charter—Hell's Angels Motorcycle Club, Boston

In the River Run Riot of April 27, 2002, several members of the Hell's Angels and the Mongols went to war. In a gambling casino, the two motorcycle clubs stabbed and shot at each other. At the end of the skirmish, Mongols member Robert Barrear was shot to death, and two Hell's Angels, Jeramie Bell and Robert Tumelty, were killed. Six members of the Hell's Angels and six members of the Mongols were sent to prison and 36 others had their charges dismissed (Vogel, 2005; Oliver, 2002).

In 1973, 11 members of the motorcycle club were sent to prison for the rape of a 16-year-old girl. In an attempt to clean up their image, the Hell's Angels Motorcycle Club members sponsored a blood drive, which was reported to be quite successful, but their crimes were not over.

Police intelligence shows that the gang members are greatly interested in weapons and have a large collection of lethal weapons. Sonny Barger was arrested and jailed in the early 1990s for plotting to bomb a rival's clubhouse. The Hell's Angels are involved in a wide variety of criminal activities including: drug trafficking, extortion, murder, prostitution, trafficking in stolen goods, etc. In San Francisco, in 2006, a dozen Hell's Angels members were arrested for a variety of crimes, including drugs, laundering monies, and using the telephone to facilitate a drug crime. The crimes would be punishable from four-year sentences to life in prison. A final disposition on all defendants includes prison sentences for all indicted, and two were sentenced to 10 years each (McEnry, 2010, personal interview).

In July 2003, 36 motorcycle club members were arrested and the club's property was seized by the federal government, ATF section, including three Hell's Angels clubhouses, $50,000 in cash, six vehicles, nine motorcycles, 600 firearms, thousands of rounds of ammunition, silencers, and varying quantities of drugs, explosives, stolen motorcycles, and suspected human skeletal remains. In Arizona, that same year, 16 members of the Hell's Angels Motorcycle Club were indicted for various violations and sent to prison for their crimes (Sanders, 2010, personal interview).

While no Hell's Angel has been arrested in the case of C4 explosives found in a cemetery in Manhattan, the Hell's Angels Motorcycle Club members remain strong suspects. There is an active ongoing investigation in this case because the Hell's Angels have a long history of using explosives in many of their crimes. A caretaker for the cemetery dug up a package of explosives wrapped in plastic bags, situated away from gravesites. Forensics personnel estimated that the package had been buried there over a year earlier. The local Hell's Angels clubhouse is located about 100 feet from the site of the explosives (Parascandola, Martinez, and Kennedy, 2010). Like other motorcycle clubs, the Hell's Angels have allies and foes within the motorcycle club subculture. Table 9.1 lists those who are allies and who are foes.

As mentioned earlier, there is not only the risk of going to jail or prison, there is also the risk of being killed in an accident or murdered by a rival gang.

- The Mongols and the Hell's Angels were at odds and it came to a head with a brawl at a gambling casino in Nevada that resulted in the deaths of 3 bikers and 13 with injuries.

Table 9.1 Allies and Rivals of the Hell's Angels Motorcycle Club

Allies	Rivals
AK81	Bandidos
Cali Cartel	Mongols
Indian Posse	Outlaws
Iron Horsemen	Pagans
	Vagos

Source: Pugmire and Covarrubias, 2006, *LA Times* article.

- Other rival motorcycle clubs harassed the Hell's Angels, including the community as well as law enforcement. In 2008, Mark "Papa" Guardado was convicted of an assault and sent to prison in Massachusetts. He also had a minor record in California. He was arrested for possession of illegal mushrooms in San Francisco (van Derbeken, 2008). He was later murdered by another rival gang member.
- Christopher Ablett turned himself in for the killing of "Papa" on October 7, 2008. A final resolution to this case has not been reached at the time of this writing.
- In 2007, a young woman was found badly beaten and sexually assaulted on the sidewalk in New York City. She was found close to a Hell's Angels Motorcycle clubhouse. No arrests have been made in this case, but the Hell's Angels remain strong suspects.

Conclusion

The Hell's Angels Motorcycle Club, along with the Outlaws Motorcycle Club, are probably the best known of the outlaw or criminal motorcycle clubs. Of course, there are others that we have deliberately not mentioned because we have chosen to concentrate on the Big Four.

In this chapter, we have seen the various kinds of crimes committed by the Outlaw Motorcycle Clubs (OMCs). Their crimes are diverse and are committed in various parts of the country. Their members are feared due partly because of the manner in which they are presented in the media. When a member is accused of a crime, the media is quick to broadcast his identity as a "Hell's Angel." When that accusation is made, immediate images are recalled, but that cannot be helped because of what is "known" about the various criminal activities of the Hell's Angels Motorcycle Club members.

Discussion Questions

1. What do you think is involved in terming a group as a 1%er group by the federal government?
2. Is there an outlaw group in your community? How criminally active are they?
3. How active are the local and federal law enforcement agencies in the fight against the outlaw groups in your community?
4. In regard to the standards for membership into the Outlaw Motorcycle Clubs, why do they have these particular standards?
5. Review the media. How many times have the Outlaw Motorcycle Gangs been depicted in the movies, TV shows, TV serials, etc.? Give examples of such movies and TV offerings.

Suggested Reading

Caine, A. 2010. *The far Mexican: The bloody rise of the Bandidos Motorcycle Club*. London: Vintage Canada.

Discussion Questions

1.

2.

3.

4.

5.

Suggested Reading

Women in Gangs

10

Introduction

When most people think about gangs, they envision large groups of young, usually African-American or Hispanic men dressed in ways that make it clear that they are members of a group. However, as we have seen throughout the earlier chapters, these images are not always correct. One of the ways that this picture is incorrect is to assume that gang members are all men. Women and young girls are gang members, too. However, while not the majority of gang members, females certainly are known to be members of gangs.

Females have been associated in some form with gangs in America since the earliest days of gangs. However, as women have seen their roles in society change in the last century, so too have we seen their roles and frequency of being involved in gangs change. Gang membership is just one of the many areas of life in which females have seen their lives change from traditional roles that primarily support men to one of similarity and equality. In the twenty-first century, the fact that females are active members of gangs is well recognized.

Females have been involved in gangs in one way or another for nearly two centuries (Nurge, 2008). However, while this fact is acknowledged in research and popular press discussions of gangs throughout time, it has only been since the 1980s that any serious or in-depth discussion of women in gangs has been available. Previously there might be a mention of females associated with a gang, but nothing more than a passing mention would be offered. Females known to be around or with gangs were typically discussed in one of three roles. First, some early research on gang-associated females presented them as "tomboys" who were seeking to be like their male counterparts, although they typically were not allowed to fully do so. Second, women found with gang members were described as either girlfriends or females not in a stable relationship, but who were providing sexual services to one or more men in the gang. Or, third, females were sometimes explained as being used by male gang members to spy on other gangs (usually by pretending to be romantically interested in a member of a competing gang), to lure unsuspecting members of rival gangs to locations where they would be assaulted and robbed, or the women were used to hold and hide guns, money, and drugs. Beyond these simple descriptions, however, there is no in-depth study of these women available prior to the last two to three decades. Consequently, there is very little known about who these women were, what they did, how they came to be associated with a gang, or anything else about their existence and gang life. In many respects, females involved with gangs were more or less "invisible" for many decades (Chesney-Lind, Shelden, and Joe, 1996).

Starting in the late 1970s and 1980s, there emerged a body of research literature that began to look seriously at who the women associated with gangs were, how they came to be so associated, and their roles and activities. What this literature revealed was that the earlier descriptions of women as girlfriends, sexual providers, and holders of illegal goods held true, but only for some of the females in and around gangs. Additionally, uncovered was the fact that some females were striving for equality in gang life and making significant progress. During this period, we began to recognize that females not only could be violent, business-oriented, and serve as both loyal and leading gang members, but, in some cases, they were doing exactly that.

Research on Females in Gangs

The most influential study of females associated with gangs in this era was Anne Campbell's book *The Girls in the Gang* (1984). In this in-depth study of young women involved in gangs in New York City during the early 1980s, Campbell revealed that the gang provided these women with a way to escape from bad homes, poverty, and what they perceived as a dead-end lifestyle. Women were joining gangs as a way to gain power, status, and independence. Being in a gang meant avoiding the stereotypical, subservient lifestyle that characterized women's lives up to that point in time. This is not to say that Campbell found women organizing or leading gangs, but they were starting to be welcomed by male gang members and were found to be occupying roles that had a much deeper involvement in gang activities than had previously been recognized.

Other early studies of women in gangs include Joan Moore's *Going Down to the Barrio* (1991), which examined both male and female Mexican gang members in Los Angeles. In this study, Moore shows that females are largely independent and autonomous from male gang members, although women were still viewed as not full members or not completely equal by their male peers. Interestingly, Moore's study suggested that women in gangs were more likely to come from more troubled homes; to be from families with alcoholic, drug-addicted, and/or criminally involved members; and to have more and more serious long-term harms come from their gang involvement.

The Number of Females in Gangs

Knowing whether there are more females in and affiliated with gangs today as compared to the past is an especially challenging task. The difficulty here is that before the 1980s, there was little attention to and mention of females in gang research, so there was no way to reliably estimate the number of females involved. The issue of whether there really are more females involved in gangs is not that important a question. As one set of observers (Maxson and Whitlock, 2002, p. 20) summarized the issue, "Regardless of whether we are reacting to an actual increase in female gang involvement or we are just not paying attention to a phenomenon that has escaped our interest for decades, it is clear that girls are joining gangs and committing sufficient crime to be of concern." Along with the idea that it doesn't matter whether there are more (or less) females in gangs today, it is also important to note that most law enforcement officials and scholars seem to be of the mindset that there are more females involved in gangs today than 100 years ago, 50 years ago, or even 30 years ago.

Community-based research suggests that in cities between 10 and 38 percent of youth self-identify as gang members (Moore and Hagedorn, 1996). Typically, a smaller proportion of girls than boys claim to be members of gangs. Viewed somewhat differently, common estimates usually suggest that about 10 percent of gang-involved persons in the United States are female (Nurge, 2008). In other cities and studies, as many as one-third of all known gang members are female (Bjerregaard and Smith, 1996; Esbensen and Winfree, 1998; Fagan, 1990; Miller, 2001a; Moore, 1991). However, the estimates are likely somewhat low due to many police departments viewing and classifying gang-affiliated females as simply troubled young women and not gang members. One way to overcome the tendency of at least some police to not classify gang-involved females as such is to look at prison inmates. A review of women in Canadian prisons shows that gang members account for fewer than 6 percent of all women incarcerated in Canada (Correctional Service of Canada, 2003). Not unexpectedly, gang-involved women are convicted of more serious, violent offenses. These women also have lower levels of education and less employment history than nongang-involved women inmates. The fact remains, though, that when official statistics from law enforcement agencies are used to estimate the proportion of gang members by sex, women are almost always reported at lower rates than in studies relying on self-reports from youth (Maxson and Whitlock, 2002). Sexism may well be a reason for the number of gang females to be undercounted.

Crimes and Delinquency of Females in Gangs

Females in gangs commit more crimes than both males and females who are not gang involved. But, gang-involved females do not have as high a level of criminal involvement (including violence) as males that are in gangs (Maxson and Whitlock, 2002). Although gang-involved females are certainly engaged in delinquent and criminal activities, including drug use, drug sales, property crimes, gun possession, and violence, they tend to be less involved than their male gang member peers (Dukes and Van Winkle, 2003; Fleisher, 1998;

Hagedorn and Devitt, 1991; Miller, 2001b; Miller and Decker, 2001). The generally lower level of delinquent/criminal involvement for gang females is a result of both structural aspects of gangs (where male members exclude females from "more serious" gang activities) and the decision of females to limit the activities they engage in to only "less serious" types of activities (Miller, 2001b; Miller and Brunson, 2000).

Research on mixed gender gangs suggests that males value the involvement of females for primarily social reasons (Miller, 2001b). This view is most common in gangs with relatively equal numbers of males and females. However, when a gang is primarily males, the few females that are involved are more likely to be seen as "one of the guys" (Miller, 2001b; see also Peterson, Miller, and Esbensen, 2001). In these instances, the females involved in the gang are more likely to be seen as and function as equal partners, with essentially the same level of involvement in delinquent and criminal activities.

Not all females who are involved in gangs are in gangs that include males. There are also all-female gangs (Lauderback, Hansen, and Waldorf, 1992; Miller, 2001b; National Youth Gang Center, 2000). However, gangs comprised of only females are not that common; the vast majority of females that are in gangs are in mixed-sex gangs (Curry, 1998; Peterson, Miller, and Esbensen, 2001). In gangs that have exclusively female membership, there is usually much less delinquent/criminal activity than is found in mixed gender or all male gangs. This fact may be related to the interesting fact that all-female gangs are more common in smaller cities and rural areas (Moore and Hagedorn, 2001). The reason for this trend is not clear, however.

Women involved in gangs are not only perpetrators of violent actions, but just as is the case with men in gangs, they are at high risk of being victims of violence (Hagedorn and Devitt, 1999; Miller, 1998; Moore, 1991). However, at the level of homicide, when gang-involved women are killed, it is typically not that they are targeted, but rather "caught in the wrong place at the wrong time" (Miller and Decker, 2001). Despite the fact that women are seemingly becoming involved in gangs in larger numbers, and their involvement has become more complete than suggested by research in the early to mid twentieth century (see Anderson, Brooks, and Langsam, 2002), there remains a fairly strong sense of sexism in gangs. Women involved in gangs are typically subjected to physical abuse, verbal harassment, and degradation and marginalization in gang activities by male gang members (Newbold and Dennehy, 2003; Miller, 2001b).

Where young women in gangs experience especially high levels of risk is in the area of sexual victimization, which is not common for men and boys in gangs. Both Miller's (2001b) and Portillos' (1996) studies of girls in mixed gender gangs clearly shows that not only are females largely viewed as sexual objects by the males in the gang, but they are frequently subjected to sexual assault. These sexual assaults come from both male members of the gang and men from rival gangs. One commonly recognized "fact" about sexual victimization of females associated with gangs is that, in order to be admitted to membership, females must engage in group sex, perhaps even having sex with all male members of the gang, in order to be initiated into the gang. While some researchers have reported that male gang members claim this to be the case, studies of female gang members dispute the truth of this claim (Decker and van Winkle, 1996).

The findings about victimization of females involved with gangs suggests that the simple fact of being involved in a gang, not necessarily what behaviors the women portray, is the factor that introduces risk of victimization. Being with male gang members is a high risk behavior for women; male gang members often victimize gang-associated women, and being with/near male gang members may put women in harm's way.

Risk Factors Associated with Females Joining Gangs

There are a wide range of issues that put females at risk when becoming gang members. Women join gangs for numerous reasons, although there are factors that are more common than others in shaping this decision. While there are common experiences and characteristics that are associated with a greater likelihood of a woman joining a gang, there are always individual and personal reasons and factors for women making this choice of joining a gang.

There are five sets of factors that are associated with increased or decreased likelihood of whether or not a girl joins a gang. These include:

1. Structural and neighborhood conditions
2. Family issues
3. Schools factors
4. Influences of peers
5. Individual factors

The first factor, structural and neighborhood conditions, focuses on the idea that, because of deteriorating living conditions and communities in urban areas, young people are raised in an environment in which there are severely restricted opportunities, poverty, and high levels of stress, tension, and violence. These conditions are likely to result in a sense of hopelessness for the future, in which the individual sees little opportunity to improve her living condition. This, in turn, leads the individual to seek ways to make her current living conditions more comfortable and safer. Here is where the gang comes in. Gangs are likely to be seen in severely depressed neighborhoods as a way to gain both social status and material goods/advantages. Young women are most likely to gravitate to a gang when there are highly visible and active gangs in the immediate vicinity of where they live (Miller, 2002).

In other words, when a gang is seen as a positive alternative to a life of poverty, victimization, and no opportunity for improvement, we should expect a girl to join a gang as a way to try to improve her life. Or, another way of viewing this is that, in socially disorganized communities, gangs may be seen as a way to achieve a structured, organized lifestyle.

A second factor is issues regarding her family. Research on this has focused on several different aspects of a youth's family life, and while there is a consistent trend showing that family issues are important, the specific aspects of family life that are associated with gang involvement vary across studies. Some studies have shown that a lack of parental involvement—specifically lower levels of parental supervision and parental attachment—is linked to the likelihood of a youth joining a gang. However, not all research supports this premise.

In addition to low levels of parental involvement, there is also a body of research that shows that a history of abuse or neglect is important in pushing young women toward gang involvement (Fleisher; 1998; Moore, 1991; Newbold and Dennehy, 2003). A study of Mexican American female gang members in Los Angeles shows that 29 percent of the young women had been sexually abused at home (Moore, 1994). Among female gang members in Hawaii, nearly two-thirds of female gang members were identified as victims of sexual abuse in their homes (Joe and Chesney-Lind, 1995). Sexual abuse may not lead a young woman directly to a gang, but she is likely to run away from home. Once on the streets, gangs become attractive alternatives to either returning home or trying to make it on one's own.

What appears to be the best explanation of how family issues influence gang involvement is that girls who join gangs are "more likely ... to come from homes with numerous problems" (Miller, 2002, p. 182). In one study (Miller, 2001b), 60 percent of gang-involved females (compared to only 24 percent of young women not involved in a gang) reported having at least three of the following five family problems: (1) having been abused by a family member, (2) violence between adults in the family, (3) alcohol abuse, (4) drug abuse, and (5) at least one family member being incarcerated. The most common of these factors is abuse (either physical or sexual) by a family member and drug addiction by a caregiver. A third common family influence on a young woman's decision to join a gang is if she has older siblings who are involved in a gang. When an older brother or sister is a gang member, the likelihood of the girl becoming involved in a gang is much higher than if she does not have gang-involved siblings (Miller, 2002). In simple terms, when a girl's family is highly dysfunctional, poor, lacks close relationships between family members, and the girl does not have a strong sense of a loving, caring, and capable family, she is more likely than her peers (who do have such a family) to be drawn to a gang.

The lack of a stable and functioning family in the lives of young women who join gangs is strong support for the common belief that gangs exist and remain in socially disorganized communities because they offer members a sense of family. The gang is often seen as a place where the individual is accepted, cared for, and provided safety, security, and both emotional and material support—the things that are commonly associated with stable and healthy families. Further evidence in support of this view is that numerous studies have shown that young females in gangs tend to join when they are young adolescents, typically before age 14 (Miller, 2002).

An interesting aspect of how family issues influence whether females are gang involved focuses not on the individual's family of origin, but instead on the young woman or girl as a mother herself. As young women, it is not uncommon for women involved in gangs to become pregnant and give birth. Much concern exists about whether gang-involved women are able to be good mothers to their children, and whether or not their gang involvement is likely to lead their children into delinquency (Fleisher and Krienert, 2004). Research on gang-involved women who become mothers shows that once women become pregnant, and especially after they give birth, they see a decrease in their level of involvement in the gang and a decrease in violent behavior (Fleisher and Krienert, 2004). Not only do young women tend to reduce their gang involvement when they become pregnant and enter motherhood, but so, too, do many girls move out of gang activities as they leave adolescence (Miller, 2001b; Moore and Hagedorn, 1996).

A third factor that is believed to be associated with girls becoming involved with a gang centers on school. This is largely as would be expected. A low level of investment in school, not succeeding in school, having low expectations for one's performance in school, and having a generally negative outlook toward school are all predictors of gang involvement for girls (Miller, 2002).

The fourth factor frequently pointed to is peer influences. Again, as is the case with the school factor, the influence of peers is as we would expect. When a girl's peers are involved in a gang, she is significantly more likely also to be involved with a gang. Also, when a girl has low self-esteem and either is socially isolated in her community or associates with peers who are delinquent, he is much more likely to be involved with a gang (Esbensen, Deschenes, and Winfree, 1999). These factors also can be seen as setting the stage for females to view a gang in a positive way. The gang as a group that provides support, friendship, "fun" activities, and a sense of belonging (e.g., being a "family" for the young woman) is attractive and a way to overcome what is missing in one's life and to provide positive rewards and feedback to the individual.

The fifth factor tends to focus on personal values. Here, we see that females who are already involved in delinquent activities are more likely to associate with gangs. Additionally, females who hold positive attitudes toward drug use and who use drugs themselves are more likely than other females to become involved in a gang (Thornberry, 1998).

Conclusion

Females belong to gangs, despite popular assumptions that gang members are only male. When females are associated with gangs, they can either be adjuncts to the males, providing support to them, assisting in gang activities and crimes, or serving in a traditional, subservient role to the men. However, as research and experience has shown in the past 40 years, females also have evolved into full-fledged gang members. In some cases, females form their own gangs, and operate independent of, or even in competition and conflict with male gangs. Or, in some cases, females are members of mixed sex gangs and operate alongside men in more or less equal roles.

Regardless of what particular roles females fulfill, and whether or not they are members of the same gangs as men, the fact remains that female gang members can be just as violent as men, and they engage in a wide variety of gang crimes. This can include violent crimes, property offenses, drug trafficking, and any type of activities that serve to bring fear to communities and power and influence to the gang (and to the members of the gang). In many ways, females have grown into an essentially equal role in the world of gangs. This means that both communities and law enforcement agencies that work to control and eliminate gangs need to be aware of women's presence.

Not only do we need to be aware of the fact that females are often associated with gangs and gang activities, but so, too, do people and organizations that work to prevent gangs and keep young people out of gangs need to be aware of how and why females are attracted to gangs. The factors that draw females to gangs are both similar to and different from the factors that attract young men to gangs. The differences in factors that both push and pull females into gang activity are factors that affect all women in our society, including a continual striving for equality and the sexual, emotional, and physical abuse. Only when we are aware of these factors and recognize some of the differences in why females join and participate in gangs can we work effectively to keep them out of gangs, and work to help them break free of the gang lifestyle.

Discussion Questions

1. How are women in gangs similar and different from men in gangs?
2. What types of criminal activities are common among women in gangs? Why are the crimes of women in gangs restricted to these types of activities?
3. Why do females join gangs? How could the known reasons for their joining be used to try to prevent them from becoming affiliated with gangs?

Prison Gangs

11

Introduction

Some of the most notorious and, perhaps most dangerous, gangs in America are those that are found in prison. Prison gangs are widely known by corrections officials (and to a lesser degree the public) to be highly organized, violent, and in control of much of the daily life in many prisons. As we will discuss later in this chapter, in some cases, gangs in prison are simply gangs from the streets that are relocated when members are arrested, convicted, and sentenced to prison for their crimes. Other times, prison gangs are created and organized by inmates who are in prison, but who were not necessarily gang members on the outside.

Prison gangs are important to understand for several reasons. First, these gangs can be very violent. Both nongang-affiliated inmates and inmates in rival gangs may be targets of assault, sexual assault, and murder by a prison gang. So, too, are prison staff frequent targets for the actions of prison gang members. Prison gangs are important to understand because they pose a strong and direct challenge to the authority and ability of prison officials and staff who control the daily life of inmates. When prison gangs engage in not only violence, but also drug smuggling and sales, making and selling of homemade alcohol, weapons, and sex, it is clear that prison gangs are dangerous. However, when a prison gang gains power in a prison (largely through violence and instilling fear in other inmates), they not only control the major forms of deviance in a prison, but they control the small issues of daily life as well. This may include what is watched on the television in dayrooms or dormitories, how much food inmates receive at meals, who can use the telephones and when, what personal possessions inmates keep, and where inmates spend their recreational time inside the prison. Clearly, prison gangs are powerful and important in the daily life of other prison inmates and the prison staff.

What Is a Prison Gang?

A prison gang is one type of dangerous inmate organization that is commonly referred to today by corrections officials as a "security threat group" (STG). This refers to "an inmate group, gang, organization, or association that has a name or identifying signs, colors, or symbols, and whose members or associates engage in a pattern of activity or departmental rule violation so as to pose a threat to the staff, to public safety, to the secure and orderly operation of a correctional institution, or to other inmates" (Schmalleger and Smykla, 2007, p. 526). A prison gang also can be defined as "any group of three (3) or more persons with recurring threatening or disruptive behavior (i.e., violations of the disciplinary rules where said violations were openly known or conferred benefit upon the group would suffice for a prison environment), including but not limited to gang crime or gang violence" (Knox, 2005, p. 2). According to the American Correctional Association, a prison gang is defined as "two or more inmates, acting together, who pose a threat to the security or safety of staff/inmates, and/ or are disruptive to programs and/or to the orderly management of the facility/system" (Knox, 2005, p. 3).

Prison gangs are not necessarily referred to as "gangs" in correctional facilities (Knox, 2005). In some jurisdictions and facilities, such groups and their members are known as "security threat groups" because they are groups that actively threaten the security of the institution. Or, in other locations, they may be referred to with the more innocuous label of a "disruptive group." Regardless of the specific terminology used, however, such groups operate on and with the same principles, goals, and behaviors that are central to the definition of a "gang." One interesting and important aspect of all of the definitions of a prison gang is that the number of inmates involved is not that important; by definition, so long as there are two or three individuals working together in pursuit of illicit or disruptive behaviors, the group meets the definition of a "prison gang." Typically, though, we think of prison gangs as comprised of larger numbers of inmates.

The first known prison gang in the United States was the Gypsy Jokers Motorcycle Club that was first recorded at the Walla Walla, Washington, penitentiary in 1950. Subsequently, gangs were identified in California prisons in 1957, and, in 1969, prison gangs were noted in Illinois. In the more than 60 years since official recognition of the first prison gang, there has been a constant (and at times growing) concern about the ways that gangs in prisons can influence day-to-day operations of the institution, and violence used both by gangs on nonmembers and between members of different gangs. Throughout these six decades, there also has been acknowledgement, by corrections officials and others, that prison gangs can be a threat to the orderly and safe operation of prisons, and that gang members are often the inmates that require the closest monitoring and most disciplinary interventions. However, while prison gangs have been recognized as present and threatening for safe and effective prison operations for many years, it is also important to note that the context of prisons and the nature and activities of gangs in prisons have changed significantly over the years. Although research on prison gangs in the mid-to-late twentieth century is informative, it is probably not that useful for working to understand and control the activities of prison gangs in the twenty-first century (Fleisher, 2006).

Prison gangs, just like their counterparts in street gangs, are a form of organized crime. This means that the gang is structured for purposes of managing business activities and making profits that benefit those who are members of the gang. On the streets, gangs earn money, which they use to finance their business operations. In prisons, actual cash money is rare, but substitutes for money, such as commissary items, privileges, drugs, cigarettes, clothing, and personal services (laundry, tattoos, sex) serve as both the commodities that are trafficked and marketed and the form of currency. The business operations of street gangs and prison gangs are essentially the same, with the important difference that, for gangs in prison, actual products/services are bought, sold, and traded, usually without the use of cash. In some ways, prisons are a model form of a "cashless economy." However, money is present in some prisons. Cash is sometimes used for prison transactions when an inmate has a person outside of prison mail money either to a second out-of-prison individual or the outsider mails money to the prison to be put into the account of an inmate to whom one is indebted.

Gangs in prison are sometimes "branches" of street gangs simply moved to prison when members are sentenced to serve time, and, at other times, prison gangs are groups that develop and emerge inside the prison (referred to as indigenous to prison). When looking at prison gangs as extensions of gangs that exist on the outside, we see the prison gang having the same organizational structure as the gang on the street, and frequently being under the direction and control of the gang leaders on the outside of prison. Most members of gangs in prison were members on the streets (Knox, 2005). According to reports by prison wardens, only about 11 percent of male prison gang members and 3 to 4 percent of female prison gang members are recruited to membership while incarcerated (Knox, 2005). When an individual who was in a leadership position in the gang on the streets enters prison, he is most likely to also occupy a leadership position in the gang in prison (Shelden, 2005).

Indigenous prison gangs are developed by inmates coming together inside of prison for purposes of both enhancing their lifestyle and seeking both a sense of belonging and protection from other inmates. Most scholars suggest that the idea of protection is the key issue in gangs developing inside of prisons (Shelden, 2005).

Some scholars have suggested that prison gang members are generally older and have a history of greater criminal involvement (Decker, 2001). This is not unexpected, however, as the members of gangs in prison are obviously those who have been identified as criminals, arrested, convicted, and sentenced to prison. And, once in prison, gang members are highly unlikely to leave their gang, meaning that as they grow older they remain members.

One very important and obvious way in which prison gangs and street gangs are similar is that race is a primary factor in the composition of gangs in both types of locations. Gangs are almost always based on racial distinctions, especially in prisons. Some gangs are exclusively Hispanics (and sometimes only certain ethnicities of Hispanics), some are only African-Americans, some are exclusively Asians, and, in the case of white supremacist gangs, only Caucasians. Although there are rare exceptions, members of prison gangs are almost always homogenous in regards to race.

Identifying the exact number of members of prison gangs is a very difficult, probably impossible task. While some members of prison gangs are open and proudly proclaim their status as aging members, for many others there is reluctance to publicly claim the label because gang members may have increased risks of being victims of attacks (as discussed below) or having their movements, privileges, and activities closely monitored and controlled by prison officials. However, based on the intelligence gathered by corrections officials, it is estimated that approximately 1 in 4 male inmates and 1 in 17 female inmates come to prison as members of gangs (Knox, 2005).

Prison gangs are believed to be present in one form or another, and to varying degrees, in all prison systems in the United States (Knox, 2005). Gangs are most likely to exist in the prisons of states that are more urban and have a greater presence of gangs on the streets. States like California, Florida, Texas, and Arizona (all of which are states with urban areas) tend to have a greater proportion of gang members among their prison populations. Smaller population states, and those without any large cities, such as North Dakota, Wyoming, Delaware, Vermont, New Hampshire, Montana, and Arkansas, do not have as serious a gang problem as larger states, although some individual gang members are in prisons in these states. A few smaller states that one might expect to be relatively gang free, however, do have a significant gang presence in prison. For instance, Idaho has a sizable number of white supremacist gang members in prison, largely because many of the Aryan movement groups and members live in Idaho.

Not surprisingly, corrections officials in higher security prisons are more likely to perceive gang members to be present in their population of inmates, and to believe that there is a greater concentration of gang members in the prison (Knox, 2000). Interestingly, though, one study of gangs in British prisons shows that staff there are most likely to identify gang activities in medium security prisons, not low or maximum security prisons (Wood and Adler, 2001).

Profiles of Prison Gangs

There are many prison gangs, some of which are very large and present in a majority of prisons across the United States, and some that are found in only one state or even only one or two specific prisons. Some gangs are chapters of larger organizations, with semiautonomous operations within specific prisons. (In this regard, prison gangs are a little bit like fraternities and sororities, where there is a national organization that establishes general rules and structures; however, chapters at individual campuses vary in their actual activities.)

One of the defining characteristics of prison gangs and their members is that these are individuals who are "extremists" (Gorowitz Institute, 2002). This means that members of prison gangs are likely to hold very strong beliefs, and their beliefs are often based on definite distinctions between what is acceptable and not acceptable, good and bad.

There is a large number of gangs found in American prisons. The National Gang Crime Research Center surveyed wardens of prisons in 49 states (Rhode Island did not participate) and identified 71 individual gangs operating in American prisons in 2004 (Knox, 2005). When looking at different gangs that were identified as present in institutions by prison wardens, the top seven gangs present in American prisons include:

1. Crips
2. Gangster Disciples
3. Bloods
4. Latin Kings
5. Vice Lords
6. Aryan Brotherhood
7. Folks

Each of these gangs is not only present in a large number of American prisons, but each also operates outside of prison, on the streets. For some gang scholars, the Aryan Brotherhood is not considered a street gang because they do not operate on the outside in the traditional ways that street gangs operate (see Chapter 1). However, even the Aryan Brotherhood is active outside of prison, although perhaps in different ways than the other (primarily African-American and Hispanic) gangs.

With the large number of gangs found in American prisons, one could devote an entire book to simply describing and discussing each gang. Because this is not possible here, and not the focus of this book, in this section we discuss seven of the most prominent, notorious, and influential gangs present in prisons in the United States. As these descriptions show, there are both common characteristics as well as some important differences among these gangs.

Bloods

The Bloods originated as a Los Angeles street gang in the 1960s in response to perceived threats from other gangs, especially the Crips. Originally known as the Pirus, the Bloods were formed out of a merging in 1972 of the Pirus and three other street gangs. As members were arrested, convicted, and incarcerated, the gang moved into California prisons and subsequently spread to Texas prisons in the 1980s. Today, the Bloods are considered one of the largest and most notorious gangs, both on the streets and in prisons, across the nation. The Bloods are centered out of Los Angeles, where they are reputed to have over 5,000 members. Chapters can be found in most major (and many mid-to-small) cities across the nation.

The Bloods are primarily an African-American gang. There are some members who are not African-American, and there is a small number of female members. The organization does not have an acknowledged national leader, but, instead, individual sets ("chapters") have their own hierarchy and leadership structure. As is well known, Bloods members identify each other through the wearing and displaying of the color red.

The Bloods do not operate on the basis of an established written charter. This is not to say that there are not established and known rules and structures, however. Because of the lack of a written charter, most corrections departments do not officially consider the Bloods to be a gang, but, instead, classify them as a "security threat group."

Aryan Brotherhood

The Aryan Brotherhood is the largest, and best known, of the white supremacist gangs in American prisons. It was originally founded in 1967 in San Quentin State Prison in California. The Aryans (including members of the Brotherhood, and other splinter groups that also are founded on Aryan principles) are based on a belief in the supremacy of white persons, and tend to follow and espouse neo-Nazi ideology. Typically, members of the Aryan Brotherhood are apolitical outside of prison, and even in prison are focused on activities to make their incarceration as comfortable as possible, and to avoid interactions and relationships with nonwhite individuals. The Aryan Brotherhood is active primarily in the Southwest and states on the Pacific coast (National Gang Intelligence Center, 2009).

Although the Aryan Brotherhood believes in the supremacy of white persons, they do coordinate some activities in prisons with other gangs, including the Mexican Mafia. However, interactions and relationships with African-American inmates and gangs are extremely rare, except in instances where African-Americans can be used to perform dangerous, high-risk actions (such as drug smuggling).

Members of the Aryan Brotherhood center their in-prison activities on drug trafficking, extortion, and activities that can make daily life more comfortable for their members. Membership in the Aryan Brotherhood is considered a life-long commitment. Full membership is believed to require a serious physical assault (including homicide) on an enemy.

The Aryan Brotherhood is only one of a large number of white supremacist prison gangs (many, although not all, of which use the term "Aryan" in
their names) (Knox, 2005). Other similar prison gangs include skinheads,
the Ku Klux Klan, White Aryan Resistance, and Aryan Nation. Two of the
common characteristics of all white supremacist prison gangs are (1) a belief
that all members share a kinship relationship, and (2) use of symbolism that
reflects a warrior culture (Etter, 2001). The warrior culture is built on a sense
of nationalism, beliefs, and values that reflect a religious orientation, racism,
and distain for nonwhites, and a fascist political philosophy. These characteristics promote loyalty to the group, and developing a strong sense of
belonging and importance of the gang for members.

White-only gangs are perhaps one of the newest concerns of prison
officials. According to a series of studies by the National Gang Crime
Research Center (see Knox, 2005), the presence of white supremacist gangs
has increased dramatically in the past 20 years. Whereas in 1991, only 27
percent of prison wardens reported the presence of separate white gangs
in their prisons, the prevalence increased to 56 percent in 1993, 70 percent in 1999, and 72 percent in 2004. The growth of separate (and typically supremacist) white gangs may be a response to the presence and threat
of African-American and Hispanic gangs, although this is difficult to say
definitively.

Black Guerrilla Family

The Black Guerrilla Family (BGF) is a primarily African-American gang that
is found across the country, although most prominently on the East and West
coasts (National Gang Intelligence Center, 2009). The BGF is a highly politically oriented gang. It operates on the basis of seeking to eliminate racism,
to maintain dignity in prison, and to overthrow the American government
(Gangs OR Us, 2009).

The BGF was founded in 1966 in the California prison system. It was
founded by George Jackson, a former Black Panther. As an outgrowth
of political activism, and having strong political goals, the Black Guerilla
Family is highly structured along paramilitary lines. The gang's organization extends to having a written national charter, an explicit code of ethics,
and an oath of allegiance, which requires a life-long commitment, with an
included death oath.

Because it works to resist (and hopefully overthrow) the American government, the BGF is highly organized and has roots in violent political activ-
ists, and it should not be surprising that it is among the most violent prison
gangs in the county. The Black Guerrilla Family is primary involved in drug
distribution. The violence perpetrated by the BGF is against other inmates
and corrections staff. Regarding their interactions with other prison gangs,

the BGF establishes allegiances and working collaborations with other African-American gangs and politically oriented groups. Because of their strong political orientation, the BGF has serious conflicts with the Aryan Brotherhood and Mexican Mafia.

Mexican Mafia

The Mexican Mafia is a Hispanic gang that focuses on maintaining ethnic solidarity and pride among members and the community. The gang was originally formed in the late 1950s in California prisons. Originally, the Mexican Mafia was formed as a street gang in Los Angeles as Mexican-American men sought to protect themselves from victimization. Today, the Mexican Mafia is found primarily in prisons in California and in the Federal Bureau of Prisons throughout the country.

The Mexican Mafia is known to be very violent, and responds quickly and violently whenever members believe they have been disrespected or crossed. The gang has a paramilitary structure with orders originating from the top and carried out by lower level, lower-status members. The "mafia" part of the gang's name reflects the fact that their structure is modeled after the Italian mafia and the fact that the gang is very disciplined, and values members disciplining deviant members.

Today the gang is primarily active in the Southwest and along the Pacific coast (National Gang Intelligence Center, 2009). The major activity of the gang is drug distribution in prison, and extorting drug distributors on the streets (National Gang Intelligence Center, 2009). When the Mexican Mafia is found in a prison that also houses members of African-American street gangs and/or the Black Guerilla Family, there tends to be a great deal of conflict between the groups.

Texas Syndicate

The Texas Syndicate, which formed in the early 1970s in California's Folsom Prison, is a gang of primarily Mexican inmates. The gang was focused on providing protection to Mexican-American inmates from the state of Texas. The inmates that formed the Texas Syndicate were being victimized by the Mexican Mafia and Aryan Brotherhood (www.gangsorus.com, 2009). Although the gang is known to be a Mexican-only gang, there are inmate members that are not Hispanic, but they are usually from Texas.

The Texas Syndicate is a highly organized organization. It has written rules that all members are expected to follow. One responsibility of membership in the Texas Syndicate is to enforce the rules on all other members. The Texas Syndicate is primarily found in Texas prisons. The gang continues to have strongly antagonistic relationships with Aryan Brotherhood and Mexican Mafia as well as La Nuestra Familia (Our Family).

Neta

The Neta is a Puerto Rican Hispanic gang that was originally founded in 1970 in Rio Pedras prison in Puerto Rico. When originally formed, the Neta was focused on attempting to stop the violence happening among inmates in the Rio Pedras prison. Today, Neta is especially prominent in the Northeast (National Gang Intelligence Center, 2009) and in Florida, where they (together with the Aryan Brotherhood) are one of the two largest prison gangs (see Florida Department of Corrections, 2009).

Neta has a strong nationalist orientation to it, and espouses a philosophy of "independence for the island" of Puerto Rico. Neta members typically view themselves as people who are being oppressed against their will by the American government. In support of their nationalist orientation, Neta use as their colors red, white, and blue (although, sometimes black is substituted for blue). Colors are often displayed in the wearing of beads, although clothing and handkerchiefs are also used as a way to proclaim membership via colors. However, Neta gang members are among the most difficult prisoners to identify and are highly unlikely to admit their membership to authorities.

Neta has strong ties to street gangs, but, inside prison, often keep a low profile, allowing other gangs (especially other Hispanic gangs) to draw the attention of officials. Neta focuses much of their activities on drug trafficking. They are violent toward both other inmates and prison staff.

Islamic Gangs

In addition to the well-known prison gangs, there are also a set of prison gangs that are based on Islamic beliefs. According to the National Gang Research Crime Center, in 2004, fully 44 percent of a national sample of prison wardens reported that they had at least one separate Islamic gang in their institution (Knox, 2005). The most commonly reported Islamic gangs in American prisons are Five Percent Nation, Nation of Islam, Fruits of Islam, the Moorish Science Temple of America, and Black Gangster Disciples.

The Black Gangster Disciples are an interesting gang to be identified as Islamic. This gang has been informed by a number of Islamic writers, speakers, and thinkers. However, examination of their internal writings does not necessarily show Islamic beliefs (Knox, 2005). Also, especially in the Illinois prisons, the Black Gangster Disciples have been known to have serious and lasting conflicts with Islamic gangs.

For Islamic gangs, there is a very strong religious aspect to their structure and operations. It is commonly believed by corrections officials that these gangs operate through and in Islamic religious organizations and activities inside of prison. This fact makes monitoring and control of Islamic gangs especially challenging for prison officials. Because of well-established legal precedents, religious groups and services enjoy a range of special protections; this means gatherings of Islamic inmates can often be unsupervised. In these ways, Islamic prison gangs can operate fairly easily and effectively in American prisons.

Structure of Prison Gangs

It is also important to note that since the turn of the century there has been something of a shift in the nature and structure of gangs in prison. In the last decade, there has been growing influence of street gangs, especially those that are not national or regional in nature and that tend to have a less-organized structure, inside American prisons. These gangs, with an increasing presence in some states' prisons, are largely the importation of street gang members to the prison setting. As larger numbers of members of street gangs get arrested, convicted, and sentenced to prison, their numbers in prison grow, and they may continue with their ways of the street, but while in prison. For these gangs, while technically they are "gangs in prison," they differ from the more common and notorious prison gangs described above in that they are less organized, more localized to specific prisons or states, and lack the far-reaching connections to other prisons and multiple sources of contraband on the outside of prison.

Identifying gang members in prison can be a challenge at times. While some gang members are well known and publicly proclaim their affiliation (as a way to build status, prestige, and power for themselves), many gang members do not publicly identify themselves (at least not to corrections officials) as members of gangs. When an inmate is known to be a gang member, he is likely to be housed in a prison or a housing unit of a prison where it is believed there are no other members of his gang. Additionally, known prison gang members (as is also the case with known members of street gangs) are watched more closely by prison officials (because they are presumed to be more likely to be "criminal" while in prison). For other prison gang members, they may not wish to proclaim their affiliation so that they are not targeted for violence by members of other gangs.

One way to identify prison gang members is by their tattoos (Valentine, 2000). Gang members, both in prison and in the community, need to be able to reliably identify other members (and know who is not a member), and while things like hand signals, code words, specific pieces of knowledge, and clothing styles may be useful, tattoos are permanent. In this way, knowing the markings of a gang can be one of the most effective ways for correctional officials to reliably know which inmates are gang members, and the specific gangs to which they belong.

However, relying solely on identifying gang members in prison by the presence of gang tattoos is not a very effective or efficient means of identification. According to a national survey of prison wardens, only a little more than one in three (38 percent) of male inmates and one in 16 (7 percent) of female inmates come to prison with tattoos that identify them as members of gangs (Knox, 2005).

Prison Gangs and Prison Culture

Inside prisons, gangs and their members occupy and fulfill a number of roles and tasks that are important to both the day-to-day and long-term culture of the institution. As we saw in the description of specific gangs, in some prisons, gangs control the market for contraband, including drugs, alcohol, weapons, cell phones, cigarettes, and anything else that is prohibited. As reported by a national sample of prison wardens, gangs do (or try to) control the black market for contraband in most prisons. Throughout the prison system, gangs control various forms of contraband: 88 percent for drugs, 45 percent for illicit sex, 56 percent for contraband food, 40 percent for contraband/extra clothing, 60 percent for loans among inmates, and 73 percent for gambling (Knox, 2005). In prison, gangs also are believed to control the extortion activities in 70 percent of prisons, and are the primary inmates involved in offering "protection" to inmates in exchange for goods/services/payment in 76 percent of American prisons.

Prison gangs also commonly control decisions about individual inmates' activities including such innocuous things as where inmates may spend their time in a housing unit, what commissary items they are allowed to purchase (and keep), what is shown on communal televisions, etc. In many respects, what this suggests is that prison gangs can be very powerful inside the culture of a prison. Although gangs do not have official or legitimate authority to control anything in prison, they use their size, threats, actual use of violence, and the fear that they instill in others to assume power and control.

Perhaps the most common way that prison gangs operate in American prisons to cloak their activities is under the cover of religion. Religious services and gatherings are generally among the least supervised activities and gatherings in prison. Due to a series of Supreme Court decisions in the latter half of the twentieth century, inmate religious activities are to be allowed and generally not interfered with by prison officials. As a result, more than two-thirds (68.8 percent) of prison wardens report that gangs use religious services as a "front" for their gathering and activities (Knox, 2005). Although all types of gangs, and gangs of all racial compositions, may use religious activities as a front for gang activities, this appears to be most common among white supremacist gangs.

Prison Gang Leaders

Leaders of prison gangs rise to their positions of power by achieving and being recognized by others (especially the members of the gang) for meeting several criteria. Important traits of gang members that contribute to high status and leadership positions include having knowledge and abilities to manage the organizational structure of the group, possessing physical strength and fighting ability, and a "reputation in the sense of notoriety" (Kobrin, Puntil, and Peloso, 1968, p. 190). Leaders of prison gangs are those who often use violence (against nonmembers and members) and are able to intimidate others. Leadership positions are not so much given to individuals as they are assumed or taken by individuals. Also, gang leaders are those who have demonstrated that they have leadership abilities; just as in any organization, it is those individuals who show that they have the knowledge and ability to organize and direct others, and to convince others to agree with them and follow them. These are the ones likely to rise in status and power.

Sandra Fortune (2003) studied prison gang leaders and describes such individuals as those that have six characteristics:

1. Demand loyalty from other members.
2. Enforce their wishes and hold their positions through instilling fear in others.
3. Able and willing to enforce their orders on others.
4. Establish a reputation for themselves among gang members.
5. Rise to their positions of power through personal connections with leaders who come before them.
6. Earn respect from others for how they conduct themselves and effectively demonstrate leadership abilities.

These characteristics are not different from leadership characteristics in any organization, with the exception that in "regular" settings and organizations, physical force and violence are typically not used. So, while the actual actions of gaining and maintaining leadership in a prison gang may differ from other settings and organizations, the actual traits are much the same. However, the central defining element of prison gang leadership is coercion of others.

Prison Gangs and Violence

Members of prison gangs are those who are most likely to be involved in violent actions within the prison (DeLisi, Bert, and Hochstetler, 2004; Ross, 2008).

One study of over 82,000 federal inmates suggests that those who are members of prison gangs are both more violent and more likely to be identified as involved in all forms of misconduct while incarcerated than nonmembers (Gaes, Wallace, and Gilman, 2002). Members of prison gangs are responsible for approximately 26 percent of violent incidents and 31.5 percent of all inmate-on-inmate violent assaults in American prisons (Knox, 2005). Even when controlling for criminal history, security level, and demographic factors, gang affiliation is the strongest predictor of which inmates are violent and likely to violate prison rules. Also, reflecting the characteristics of prison gang leaders described above, those members who are more "embedded" (or closer to the high status power/leadership positions in the gang) are those who are most likely to be violent while in prison.

Prison gang members typically use violence and the threat of violence as their way of enhancing their status, gaining goods and services from others, and recruiting new members (Ross, 2008). When a prison gang seeks to draw a new inmate into membership, they may use violence against the individual to show him that he needs to be a member of the gang so as to avoid being continually victimized. In a somewhat ironic approach to recruiting new members, the prison gang may harm the individual they seek to recruit, rather that woo him; recruitment often centers on scaring an individual into joining rather than enticing him to do so (Ross, 2008).

Gang members in prison are a threat not only to other inmates, but to correctional staff as well. One national study of correctional officials reports that in the previous year a staff member was physically assaulted by at least one gang member in about one-sixth of all American prisons (Knox, 2000). A study of prison gang members in North Carolina reports that prison gangs are more likely than street gangs to target "authority figures" (such as prison staff) for violence than are street gangs (Jackson and Sharpe, 1997). This should not come as a surprise, however, since in prison the authority figures have a much greater degree of control over the everyday and minute aspects of gang members' activities than do law enforcement officers on the streets. Prison gang members are in more frequent and closer contact with authority figures than street gang members, who are able to avoid constant contact with such types of authorities.

Members of prison gangs do assault staff, although not as frequently or in numbers as high as many outside observers might expect. According to the National Gang Crime Research Center, national surveys with prison wardens show that only one in five (20.4 percent) of prison wardens report gang assaults on staff as a problem in their prison (Knox, 2005). However, when prison gang members do physically assault staff members, these tend to be serious assaults and result in significant injuries. More common than physical assaults are threats of assault on staff; one in three (33.7 percent) of prison wardens report that gang members threaten staff. This clearly shows that prison gangs are a danger not only to other inmates, but also to those who operate American prisons.

Finally, it is worth noting that prospects for the future in regards to the presence, power, and activities of prison gangs are not very bright. Not only have prison gangs gained in prominence and power over the past few decades, but prison wardens also predict that such growth will only continue. The national study of prison wardens conducted by the National Gang Crime Research Center (Knox, 2005) reports that more than 70 percent of wardens expect the problem of inmate gang violence will get worse in the coming years and 27 percent believe the problem will stay at its current level. Despite their best efforts to control and minimize the presence and activities of prison gangs, only 2.6 percent of wardens see progress being made and gangs becoming less of a problem.

How Prison Officials Work to Control Prison Gangs

Rather obviously, one important goal for corrections administrators is to control the activities of gangs in prisons. With the primary goal of prison administrators being to provide a safe and humane facility in which convicted offenders are housed (and hopefully rehabilitated), it is critical that the activities of criminal groups well-known for violence, intimidation, and control of economic black markets in the institution be monitored and controlled. While at first glance it might appear that this would be a relatively easy task, after all, prisons are places where inmates never leave and staff can watch them 24 hours a day, 7 days a week; in fact, it can be very challenging to know who is a member of a prison gang, what the gang is doing, and when a gang is most likely to attack other inmates or staff. Therefore, the importance of vigilance in watching, listening, and responding quickly is even more important. The importance of working to control gangs also can be seen in the fact that fully two-thirds of American prisons have at least one staff person whose full-time job is to coordinate intelligence and monitor prison gangs and their members (Knox, 2005).

The most common methods of attempting to control and eliminate gangs in prisons have been to segregate known gang members, to enforce extended lockdowns of prisons (so as to eliminate opportunities for inmates to move and communicate), and transferring inmates between prisons (Fleisher and Decker, 2001). The idea of placing gang members in segregation and attempting to limit their contact and interactions with others, however, is generally seen by corrections officials as a weak and ineffective means of controlling gangs (Knox, 2000). Additionally, in as many as one-half of all prisons, administrators report that they attempt to develop intelligence about the activities of gangs in the prison through the use of informers (e.g., "snitches"), as well as closely monitoring gang members' mail and telephone calls (Shelden, 2005).

The practice of transferring gang member inmates is a practice known as dispersion. This idea is based on the belief that, when gang members are concentrated in one or only a few prisons, they are able to hold power because of their numbers (e.g., the idea of "there is power in numbers"). In an attempt to counteract this situation, corrections officials may seek to disperse members of gangs across prisons, both within the state and sometimes to prisons in other states. When a prison has relatively equal numbers of members of different prison gangs (as opposed to one gang having a much larger number), it is less likely that any particular gang can and will have significant power/control in that prison.

One of the potential problems with a dispersion approach to controlling prison gangs is that some states do not have many prisons, so it is not possible to spread the members of gangs out over multiple facilities. A way to overcome this problem is for departments of corrections in different states to trade inmates with one another. If state A has a large number of Aryan Brotherhood members, but only three prisons, and neighboring state B has a large number of Mexican Mafia members (but few Aryans), state A may agree to send Aryans to state B and in exchange take Mexican Mafia members into their prisons. In this way, although the total number of gang members does not decrease, the members of particular gangs are dispersed across more prisons, inhibiting them from gaining a power base in any specific prison.

When gangs are present in a prison and it is not possible to control their numbers via dispersion or other methods, it is incumbent on corrections officials to find ways to limit the influence of gangs on prison culture and operations. There are a number of approaches that corrections officials may use to try to control the activities of prison gangs and their members. Some of these are focused on individuals already known to be gang members, some are focused on attempting to stop the recruitment of new gang members, and some activities are attempts to limit the violence and other problems that are common with gang members in prisons. The more common control activities that are used by prison officials include:

- Observing inmates' daily routines in an effort to identify gang networks and activities.
- Transferring known gang members to other (usually higher security level) prisons.
- Limiting inmates' access to money or other items of value, so as to try to control gangs' influence on the informal economy of the prison.
- Segregating gang leaders and the most violent gang members from the general population of the prison.

- Recruiting informers from the inmate population.
- Developing intelligence through a special unit of prison officers.

In almost all prisons in the United States there are today intelligence units or officers whose responsibility it is to gather information and develop approaches for controlling the activities of gang members. Although intelligence units spend a great deal of their time on gang issues, they are not limited to working on only gang problems. Intelligence unit officers also focus on nongang member violent inmates and all other types of potentially disruptive inmates. Included in the types of activities that intelligence unit members in prisons do are:

- Developing confidential informants in the inmate population
- Infiltrating gangs through undercover work
- Opening and monitoring inmates' incoming and outgoing mail
- Monitoring telephone calls from inmates
- Reviewing new inmates for gang members
- Plugging security breaches when they are found

One means by which many observers believe that prison gangs can be somewhat controlled is for prison officials to explicitly prohibit gangs from recruiting new members. However, only 75 percent of prison wardens report that their institution/system has a rule that specifically prohibits existing gangs from trying to recruit new members (Knox, 2005). The fact that fully one-quarter of prisons do not have rules against recruitment may simply be a recognition that having a rule is not unlikely to be effective; after all, when trying to control the activities of a criminal, disruptive, rule-breaking group of inmates, putting a rule in place is not very likely to be effective. This point is recognized by corrections officials. Nearly all (94 percent) prison wardens report that gangs in their institutions do recruit new members. So, even in the three-quarters of prisons where recruitment is not allowed, it continues to occur.

Prison gangs can and do recruit new members not only in the prison where specific recruiting members are housed, but also across institutions. Because nearly one-half of prisons allow inmates in one prison to communicate with inmates in other institutions (via the U.S. mail), there can be a fair amount of gang business (including recruitment and intimidation for purposes of recruitment) conducted between prisons. This is an area where the law generally allows corrections officials to restrict inmates' activities, but in only about one-half of institutions is it restricted.

One approach in trying to control the activities of gangs that has been shown to be ineffective is for prison officials to view gangs as an interest group with whom they can negotiate and try to work out agreements that will keep the gang (relatively) nonviolent and not disruptive. Most (70 percent) of prison wardens responding to surveys from the National Gang Crime Research Center report that attempting "to bargain with an inmate gang leader (is) similar to negotiating with terrorists" (Knox, 2005). While in the 1970s such an approach was fairly common, and even a standard part of a prison warden's tasks, today such an approach is seen as something "you should not do" (Knox, 2005, p. 10).

Conclusion

Clearly, prison gangs are important and influential components of prison culture and operations. They are by no means new developments, but, in fact, have had for many decades large and important impacts on how prisons operate. Although how a prison gang is defined is something that lacks a clear and universally accepted answer, the fact remains that gangs in prisons are fairly common, are violent, and are important challenges for administrators who operate prisons.

Prison gangs are very similar to gangs on the streets. In fact, many prison gangs (but certainly not all) are extensions of gangs outside of prison. Prison gangs are often highly organized, distinguished by race, and involved in a wide range of deviant, criminal, and violent activities.

Discussion Questions

1. What are the major prison gangs in the United States and how do they differ from one another?
2. What types of criminal and/or deviant activities are common to prison gangs?
3. Outline and discuss the arguments about whether prison gangs are imported to the prison environment or emerge in response to it.
4. In what ways, both positive and negative, do prison gangs influence the culture of a prison?
5. What types of violence do prison gangs engage in? How does this activity influence the daily life of other inmates and prison staff?
6. Explain the various approaches correctional institutions use to try to combat the presence and harm of prison gangs. Which methods are more or less effective?

Gang Policy

12

Policy to control gangs and gang life is complex. A substantial number of policies have been developed in an attempt to reduce the issues that come with gangs. In an effort to present the themes that are central to these policies, we categorize them based on whether they are community-oriented or legally oriented. Within these categories, a number of typologies may be presented to better understand the policies that exist in the community or legal environments.

Community Policies

A number of community policies have been used to reduce instances of gangs and gang life.

Spergel and Curry's Developmental Community Interventions

Spergel and Curry (1990), two University of Chicago sociologists, surveyed a number of criminal justice and community agencies in over 40 cities. The results of their study show a typology of cities that was based on the extent of gang activity in the cities. Spergel and Curry identified two varieties of cities that were based on the degree of gang problems present in the communities. They referred to the first variety as *chronic* gang problem cities and the other as *emerging* gang problem cities. Chronic gang problem cities have had gang problems for several years, whereas, cities with emerging gang problems are those with only recent gang problems. This typology becomes important when trying to understand the effectiveness of various community interventions that are being used to reduce gang issues. In addition to providing the typology for gangs, Spergel and Curry argued that four broad areas might be used to understand the community interventions:

1. Community organization
2. Social intervention
3. Opportunities provision
4. Suppression

From the Spergel and Curry survey, the cities have used these four main strategies.

Community Organization

This area is concerned with the relationships of the groups in the community. Spergel and Curry (1990) argued that networking among various groups and organizations would help the community cope with gang issues. An important element of community organization is communication to ensure that services are not duplicated. The services that the organizations provided were designed to promote trust, mobilize the community, provide education (especially for parents and children), and the development of community groups (children and parents).

Social Intervention

Social interventions are designed to help counsel youth about problems, with a focus on guiding youth away from gang involvement. This area was designed to help mold and shape the values of youth to a point where gangs are not an issue. The main technique used in social interventions is youth outreach and counseling strategies.

Opportunities Provision

This area of intervention focuses on creation of opportunities. This creation includes jobs and education. Spergel and Curry (1990) argued that this area was used to target at-risk youth, who could become gang members, in an effort to help them improve their educational skills and train for jobs.

Suppression

This policy area is primarily concerned with reducing gangs and the advantages of gang life. Spergel and Curry (1990) argued that this was primarily the criminal justice system's, especially police, response to gangs and gang life. This response included tactical changes to better monitor and control gangs. For instance, some of these tactics include the development of police gang units, specialized patrols, legislation that targets gang activity, and better information systems. (See Chapter 3 for more details on these types of efforts.)

Effectiveness of These Policies

Spergel and Curry (1990) asked their respondents to rank the effectiveness of these strategies. To that end, the determination of effectiveness coming from their study is based on opinion. Nevertheless, the results are rather instructive. On one hand, the respondents from chronic gang problem cities rank the effectiveness of policy areas as: (1) community organization, (2) opportunities provision, (3) social intervention, and (4) suppression. On the other hand, the respondents from emerging gang problem cities rank the importance and effectiveness of policy areas as: (1) opportunities provision, (2) community organization, (3) suppression, and (4) social intervention. A word of caution is necessary when interpreting these rankings. This is not to imply that only one form of policy area may be important in reducing gangs and removing the advantages of gang life. Further, it is important to stress that Spergel and Curry argued that these policy areas may work best in conjunction with each other. To be clear, a policy implemented from each of the areas at the same time may be effective in reducing gangs and the advantages of gang life. Thus, from these results, it is not clear the types of policies that truly are effective. Perhaps other methods of viewing policies may provide more insight into how to reduce gangs and gang life.

A Risk-Focused Approach

The risk-focused approach is designed to prevent an issue before it begins (Hawkins, Catalano, and Miller, 1992). The best method to prevent a problem is to understand the factors that are likely to lead to a problem. According to Hawkins et al., these risk factors include: (1) community, (2) family, (3) school, and (4) individual/peers. Important methodology issues that would relieve the factors likely to lead to a problem (i.e., protective factors) include: (1) individual characteristics, (2) bonding, and (3) healthy beliefs and clear standards.

Individual Characteristics

Four main individual characteristics are important for staying away from gangs: (1) gender, (2) resilient temperament, (3) perceived social orientation, and (4) intelligence. Gender is an important characteristic because it refers to the social role of the individual. In the context of gangs and gang life, as elaborated upon in Chapter 1, males are more likely than females to join gangs (Spergel, 1995). This comes from the gender-role socialization. For instance, males are socialized to be aggressive and females are socialized to be less aggressive and more congenial.

Resilient temperament is the ability to overcome adversity and to be less likely to be delinquent and join gangs (McGloin, 2007). A positive social orientation of being friendly and good humored is associated with being less likely to join gangs (Brownfield, 2010). Youth that have a high level of intelligence are also less likely to be delinquent and join gangs.

Bonding

Individuals that have a close relationship or connection with others have strong bonds (Hirschi, 1969). Youth with strong bonds with family, teachers, and others are less likely to become delinquent. Youth that come from strongly bonded households are less likely to become delinquent, even when they reside in at-risk neighborhoods. Brownfield (2010) showed that those with stronger bonds were less likely to become gang members.

Healthy Beliefs and Clear Standards

Bonds are only important when the object of the bond is prosocial. To be clear, individuals that have strong bonds with someone that is involved with a gang is likely to be involved with a gang as well and vice versa (Hawkins, Catalano, and Miller, 1992). Thus, bonds need to be with healthy or prosocial individuals to be effective in preventing youth from becoming involved in gangs. These individuals will have clear standards that criminal and delinquent activity is not proper behavior.

Examples of Community Policies and Programs to Reduce Gangs and Gang Life

A number of initiatives have been undertaken to reduce gang involvement. Some of the specific policies or programs are presented below. The programs share some commonalities in their goals, but have different methods of achieving these goals. For instance, many of the programs provide education about violence prevention in community-based situations. Other programs are more focused on recreational activities. The tactics that these programs use often overlap. What is important is that these programs must always deal with continual changes in funding, including vacillation from underfunding to overfunding. Further, these programs have to deal with high employee turnover, low employee morale, and bureaucratic red tape. Some of these programs are governmental priorities, and some have roots in the community, religious institutions, and/or the criminal justice system.

One style of program provides social work, counseling, and tutoring, for example Boy Scouts, Boys and Girls Clubs, and others (Goldstein, 1993). These programs are based on social work types of counseling and the theory that the programs should be brought to the gang youth. The programs consist of control efforts, treatment, education, and changes in values. Unfortunately, they have not been very effective in reducing gang involvement (Goldstein, 1993).

Another variety of program that has been used to address issues of gang involvement are opportunity-oriented. These attempt to address problems that are central to the lives of gang members, such as unemployment, low wages, lack of recreational and educational opportunities, poor health, and inadequate housing (Goldstein, 1993; Spergel and Curry, 1990). Examples of these types of programs can be found all across the country and they have two general sections in their structure. The first is prevention, which emphasizes the identification of at-risk youth for gangs. The second is remediation that targets members of gangs for intervention. While these two are identifiable, most of the programs seem to emphasize prevention (Goldstein, 1993; Spergel and Curry, 1990). To address prevention, the programs generally use two tactical approaches: (1) classroom sessions (i.e., addressing issues in discussion sessions), and (2) after-school programs (i.e., athletics and recreational activities) (Goldstein, 1993).

A number of programs may be seen as preventative. For instance, Children At Risk (CAR) (Drowns and Hess, 1995) is a diversion program. That is, CAR moves at-risk youth through a number of intensive programs and activities so that the youth stay busy. Other forms of these programs include: Save Our Sons and Daughters, The Mothers of All Children, Mothers against Violence in America, and Gang Prevention through Targeted Outreach. The activities of these programs include case management, after-school and summer programs, tutoring, mentoring, and community expectations.

Another set of programs is designed to help at-risk youth learn more about community expectations. For instance, one such program that shows youths how to care about their neighborhood is Operation Kids Care about Neighborhoods (Drowns and Hess, 1995). The youth in this program assist in cleaning the neighborhood as well as attending a number of classroom lessons. Other programs that help show youths how to care about their neighborhoods are the Garden Project and the Optimist Club.

Some programs operate within the structure of the gang. Specifically, these programs were designed to help the gang members identify with the community that they live in. This allows the gang members to gain a full appreciation of the types of standards that are proper for their community. One program of interest here is Aggression Replacement Training (Goldstein and Glick, 1994). Another program operated under a similar structure is the Pro-Social Gang Project.

The above mentioned programs are not a complete listing of the types of policies and programs that have been used or that are being used to reduce gangs and gang life throughout communities, but are merely examples of programs that have been implemented. Oftentimes such programs are relatively short-lived (due most often to funding problems). Numerous other examples can be found in most American cities. At this point, we turn to a discussion of the legal policies and interventions that have been used in the United States to address gang problems.

Legal Policies

Three parts of the criminal justice system have policy relevance for gangs and gang life. Here, we focus on policing, prosecution, and legislatures. Chapter 3 discussed a number of law enforcement efforts to address gangs, and here we return to this discussion, focusing on some different aspects of the policing approach.

Policing

The police carry out a number of functions that provide safety and security to a community, state, or nation. Law enforcement is one of the tasks that is usually performed by the police at the local, state, or the federal levels (i.e., Federal Bureau of Investigation, Department of Homeland Security, state police, county sheriffs, etc.). Other tasks that police perform are order maintenance, service, and the implementation of various legal mandates. Order maintenance refers to the actions that the police do to reduce, prevent, or stop behavior that threatens or disturbs the peace and security of a community, including face-to-face conflicts among community members. Service refers to the police assisting the public in a variety of ways that usually do not relate to crime. Implementation of a mandate is carrying out the wishes of a law or the public. These functions are instrumental in how police suppress gang activity.

The police have implemented a number of law enforcement activities to reduce instances of gangs and gang life. For instance, some police departments have developed specialized gang units. These units have several tasks that they must perform (Anderson and Dyson, 1996). One task is the identification of criminal youth and their leaders. Another task is to collect, analyze, and disseminate information that is related to the group. Also, the units investigate and gather intelligence about the group (Etter, 2001). Further, they perform surveillance, primarily of youth groups (Etter, 2001). These specialized units have a substantial amount of responsibility related to maintaining public safety. So much responsibility is given to these units that they usually develop subunits for each of the tasks mentioned above. These units are generally in large metropolitan areas that have what Spergel and Curry (1990) call chronic gang problems.

The police also have used other tactics to suppress gang activity. One of these tactics is through programs. Two notable programs—DARE (Drug Abuse Resistance Education) and GREAT (Gang Resistance Education and Training)—are instructive to the efforts of the police throughout the United States. The core of DARE was originally developed in 1983 in the Los Angeles Unified School District. In this program, specially trained police officers teach a drug use prevention curriculum in elementary, middle/junior, and high schools. The curriculum consists of 17 lessons that are usually offered once a week for 45 to 60 minutes using lectures, group discussions, question-and-answer sessions, audiovisual material, workbook exercises, and role-playing. The information in this curriculum is more than just about drugs — it also contains information on decision-making skills, self-esteem, and choosing healthy alternatives to drugs. Although not specifically focused on gang issues, by focusing on decision making, self-esteem, and drugs, it is believed that many youth will be diverted from becoming gang involved.

GREAT is a program that the police use specifically for gang activity (Esbensen and Osgood, 1999). In this program, youth are taught skill training, and information that pertains to self-esteem, peer pressure, violence, and gangs. This is designed to be covered in a classroom format by uniformed police officers to sixth and seventh graders over an eight-week period.

Prosecution

The prosecutor's office or the individual prosecutor brings a number of different types of disputes to the attention of the courts. Three types are important for the courts: (1) private disputes (civil matters), (2) public defendant disputes (holding government officials and agencies accountable), and (3) public-initiated disputes (holding potential offenders accountable) (Fox and Lane, 2010). The prosecutor is the regulator of this portion of the criminal justice system for disputes of the second and third variety (Vago, 1994). The prosecutor has the ability to support law enforcement by asking for investigations for the various disputes or prosecuting the cases that law enforcement brings to them (Vago, 1994). The prosecutor does not have any direct legislative or regulatory power, but does have a substantial amount of discretion in what cases they pursue and how they choose to do so.

Prosecutors use their discretion in two ways. One way is in deciding whether to prosecute individuals involved in a particular dispute. Prosecutors consider the severity of the offense, public sentiment about the nature and severity of the offense, and the strength of the evidence available to "prove" their case (Guagliardo and Langston, 1997). When a prosecutor decides to prosecute a case, he/she usually approaches the case with a substantial amount of vigor. Another way that prosecutors use their discretion is in not prosecuting a case. Prosecutors may decide not to prosecute a particular case of offender for several reasons: (1) the evidence in the case is not considered strong or substantial enough to likely result in a conviction, (2) the cost of prosecution is too high, (3) the offender is capable of assisting other enforcement goals, and (4) the offender may be handled in a way considered more appropriate without prosecution (Guagliardo and Langston, 1997; Fox and Lane, 2010).

Prosecutors can be instrumental in combating youth gangs and gang members (Genelin, 1993). Prosecutors use existing laws or employ new gang statutes (Fox and Lane, 2010). For example, prosecutors may be able to seize property (e.g., weapons), impose liability, file charges (such as those related to drug trafficking or vandalism charges), and file enhancements. These are important tools prosecutors use to help reduce gangs and the residue from gang life.

Legislature

Legislatures have the task of developing laws (i.e., legislation) for their jurisdictions. These laws are to be developed within constitutional confines of both the United States and the specific state in which they operate. All states in the United States, except Nebraska, have bicameral governments (Dye, 2007). This means the legislature is housed in two separate but collaborating units of government (i.e., House of Representatives or Senate). The individuals that make these laws are called legislators. Another way of describing legislators is either as representatives or senators. A legislator's job is to work with other legislators to make our laws.

In the context of gangs, legislators have had to deal with a multitude of issues. First, legislators have had to contend with politics. Politics is important because it defines the environment in which a legislator must work. One environment is the legislator's political party (Dye, 2007). A political party is a group that carries similar beliefs and generally agrees to work together. An example of a criminal justice issue that has been highly political is the legislator's stance on crime. Most often, legislators from the Republican party have taken a hard line toward toughness on crime. One method that has been effective in making sure that this is an important stance has been the masterful use of scare tactics through the media. For example, in the 1988 Presidential election, George H. Bush's campaign worked to make a mockery out of the Democratic candidate, Michael Dukakis, because of what was interpreted as Dukakis's compassion for criminals. While serving as Governor of Massachusetts, Dukakis allowed an inmate out of prison on a work furlough. During this time, the inmate raped and killed a woman. The Bush campaign used this as a method of scaring the public and emphasizing that Dukakis was weak on crime. Subsequently, George H. Bush won the presidency over Michael Dukakis.

Second, legislators have had to face important issues concerning the definition of a gang (Klein, 1995). Like others (i.e., social scientists), legislators have had difficulty defining a gang or being able to describe what a gang may look like. The issue here is that not being able to effectively define a gang makes writing laws about them difficult. To avoid the difficulty of writing laws specific to gangs and avoiding the stance of being perceived as being weak on crime, legislators have generally worked to develop creative sanctions for specific actions that are illegal. These sanctions may or may not be directed at gangs.

One example of this type of legislation was the use of enhancements (McCorkle and Meithe, 2001). Enhancements are additional penalties depending on the circumstances of crimes. In some jurisdictions, legislation has been passed that specifically uses the term *gangs* in their enhancements. That is, the laws allowed for additional penalties if law enforcement deemed that the action was performed by a gang. One piece of legislation that followed this model was RICO (Racketeer Influenced and Corrupt Organization) laws. RICO laws were designed for racketeering types of offenses that are generally attributed to organized crime, such as the Mafia. These laws allow the government to seize property because of involvement with a gang and include additional prison time added to sentences for convicted offenders. Other types of legislation that used enhancements include Wisconsin's The Street Gang Crime Act. This law allowed for additional penalties for gang types of activities (e.g., drive-bys) or allowed for double penalties for gang-related types of activities. Another form of this type of legislation is the three-strikes legislation. These laws were designed to provide prosecutors and judges with the tools to remove repeat, serious, and especially violent offenders off the streets. For instance, an individual that is being tried for a felony may be given a strike. The use of the strikes is determined by the prosecution or judges. When the individual has a criminal record that shows he/she has been convicted of a third strike, the offender is "out" (of society), and sent to prison for an extended period—sometimes life. The wisdom and consequences of three strikes legislation, however, has been vigorously debated since such laws were enacted.

Some laws have taken a different approach, which has been to focus directly on the gangs. This means that they did not use enhancements, but rather these laws were developed from deep-seated fears about gangs and gang life. These laws come about from the violent stereotypes that have been portrayed by law enforcement and the media. This led California to enact The Street Terrorism Enforcement and Prevention Act (STEP). This law treated gangs as though they were terrorists. This means that STEP was written in a way where gangs were thought to be highly organized with strong leadership. To some extent, STEP was written to treat gangs not only as terrorists, but as organized crime groups that would be akin to the Mafia.

Conclusion

Reducing gangs is an important issue because of the havoc that they may generate. Two types of policies that may be used in this area are community and legal. Community policies focus on reducing the gang activity in the community through community-based programs. A wide range of community efforts have been developed and implemented in American cities focusing on community organization, opportunities provisions, and suppression. Within the range of community-based policies, a risk-focused approach may be used to reduce instances of gang violence. This approach focuses on individual characteristics, bonding, healthy beliefs, and clear standards. The second type of policy, legal strategies, includes policing strategies and programs such as DARE and GREAT. Legal strategies also include prosecution decisions to emphasize gang reduction and legislation to reduce instances in gang activity.

Discussion Questions

1. Explain the differences between community and policing responses to gangs and gang life.
2. What are the individual characteristics of gangs and gang life? How do they work?
3. Discuss the risk-protective approach to reducing gangs and gang life.
4. Explain Hirschi's (1969) view on gangs and how it enriches Hawkins, Catalano, and Miller's (1992) risk-protective approach to gangs.

References

Adler, P. and P. Adler. 1994. *Women in outlaw motorcycle clubs, from constructions of deviance: Social power, context, and interaction.* New York: Aldine.

Alderden, M. and T. Lavery. 2007. Predicting homicide clearances in Chicago: Investigating disparities in predictors across different types of homicides. *Homicide Studies.* 11: 115–132.

Allender, D. 2001. *Gangs in middle America.* FBI Law Enforcement Bulletin. Washington, D.C., 1–9.

Anderson, E. 1999. *Code of the streets.* New York: W. W. Norton.

Anderson, J. and L. Dyson. 1996. Community strategies to neutralize gang proliferation. *Journal of Gang Research* 3: 17–26.

Anderson, J., E. Brooks, and A. Langsam. 2002. The "new" female gang member: Anomaly or evolution? *Journal of Quantitative Criminology* 10: 47–65.

Associated Press. 2009. 8 deaths in Canada linked to biker gang: Five people arrested on murder chargers. www.nicaso.com/pages/doc_page210.html (Retrieved on December 6, 2010); *National Pagans Motorcycle Club* (October 7). (Retrieved on December 10, 2010).

Bach, L. 2002. Motorcycle gang violence. Laughlin turns deadly. *Las Vegas Review.* Las Vegas: p. 1. (Retrieved August, 29, 2010).

Barker, T. 2005. One percent biker clubs—A description. In *Trends in Organized Crime.* Berlin: SpringerLink, 111.

Barker, T. and K. Human. 2009. Crimes of the Big Four Gangs. http://www.ncjrs.gov/app/publications/abstracts.aspx?=248772 (Retrieved July 29, 2011).

Barger, S., K. Zimmerman, and K. Zimmerman. 2001. *Hell's Angel: The life and times of Sonny Barger and the Hell's Angels Motorcycle Club.* New York: Harper Collins.

Bjerrgaard, B. and C. Smith. 1996. Gender differences in gang participation, delinquency, and substance use. *Journal of Quantitative Criminology* 9: 329–355.

Block, C. and A. Christakos. 1995. *Major trends in Chicago homicide: 1965–1994.* Chicago: Criminal Justice Information Authority.

Block, R. and C. Block. 1993. *Street gang crime in Chicago. Research in brief.* Washington, D.C.: U.S. Department of Justice, National Institute of Justice.

Braga, A., J. McDevitt, and G. Pierce. 2006. Understanding and preventing gang violence: Problem analysis and response development in Lowell, Massachusetts. *Police Quarterly* 9: 20–46.

Brandt, G. and B. Russell. 2002. Differentiating factors in gang and drug-related homicide. *Journal of Gang Research* 9: 23–40.

Brownfield, D. 2010. Social control, self-control, and gang member. *The Journal of Gang Membership* 17: 1–12.

Caine, A. 2009. *Befriend and betray: Infiltrating the Hell's Angels and other criminal brotherhoods.* New York: Macmillan.

Caine, A. 2010. The far Mexican: The bloody rise of the Bandido Motorcycle Club. Mississauga, Ontario: Vintage Press.

Campbell, A. 1984. The girls in the gang: April report from New York City. Cambridge, MA: Blackwell.

Carlie, M. 2002. Into the abyss: A personal journey into the world of the street gangs. New York: Asian Books.

Chatterjee, J. 2007. Gang prevention and intervention strategies. Ottawa, Ontario: Research and Evaluation Branch, Royal Canadian Mounted Police.

Chesney-Lind, M., R. Shelden, and K. Joe. 1996. Girls, delinquency, and gang membership.I In C.R. Huff (ed.), Gangs in America, 2nd ed. (pp. 185–204). Thousand Oaks, CA: Sage Publications.

Chin, K. 1990. Chinese subculture and criminality: Non-traditional crime groups in America. Westport, CT: Greenwood.

Chin, K. 1996. Gang violence in Chinatown. In C.R. Huff (ed.), Gangs in America, 2nd ed. (pp. 157–184). Thousand Oaks, CA: Sage.

Cohen, J., J. Cork, J. Engberg, and G. Tita. 1998. The role of drug markets and gangs in local homicide rates. Homicide Studies 2: 241–262.

Correctional Services of Canada. 2003. April profile of women gang members in Canada. Ottawa, Ontario: Correctional Services of Canada Research Branch.

Curry, D., R. Ball, and R. Fox. 1994. Gang crime and law enforcement record keeping. Washington, D.C.: National Institute of Justice.

Curry, G. 1998. Female gang involvement. Journal of Research in Crime and Delinquency. 35: 100–118.

Curry, G. and S. Decker. 1998. Confronting gangs: Crime and community. Los Angeles: Roxbury Press.

Decker, S. 2001. From the streets to the prison: Understanding and responding to gangs. Indianapolis: National Major Gang Task Force.

Decker, S. and B. Van Winkle. 1996. Life in the gang: Family, friends and violence. New York: Cambridge University Press.

Delaney, W. 2005. A brief history of outlaw motorcycle clubs. International Journal of Motorcycle Studies. November: 33–37.

Delisi, M., M. Berg, and A. Hochstetler. 2004. Gang members, career criminals and prison violence. Further specifications of the importation model of inmate behavior. Criminal Justice Studies. 17: 369–383.

Denson, B. 2008. Police fear violence as outlaw bikers move to Oregon. Oregon News, April 20, A-1.

Dobyns, J. 2009. No angel: My harrowing undercover journey to the inner circle of the Hell's Angels. New York: Crown.

Drew, A. 2002. The everything motorcycle book: The one book you must have to buy, ride, and maintain your motorcycle. Avon, MA: Adams Media Corp.

Drowns, R. and K. Hess. 1995. Juvenile Justice. Belmont, CA: Sage Publications.

Dukes, S. and B. Van Winkle. 2003. Gender and gang membership: April contract of rural and urban youth on attitudes and behavior. Youth and Society 34: 415–440.

Dulaney, W. 2005. A brief history of outlaw motorcycle clubs. International Journal of Motorcycle Studies 3: 5–7.

Duran, R. 2009. Legitimate oppression: Inner-city Mexican American experiences with police gang enforcement. Journal of Contemporary Ethnography 38: 143–168.

Dye, T. 2007. *Understanding public policy.* Upper Saddle River, NJ: Prentice Hall.

Edwards, P. 2009. Accused killer a "monster." thestar.com, Ontario, Canada, pp. 1–14.

Esbensen, F. and E. Deschenes. 1998. A multisite examination of youth gang membership: Does gender matter? *Criminology* 36: 799–828.

Esbensen, F. and T. Winfree. 1998. Race and gender differences between gang and non-gang youth. Results from a multisite survey. *Justice Quarterly* 15: 505–526.

Esbensen, F. and D. Osgood. 1999. Gang Resistance Education and Training (G.R.E.A.T.). Results from the National Evaluation, *Journal of Research in Crime and Delinquency* 26: 194–25.

Esbensen, F., E. Deschenes and T. Winfree. 1999. Differences between gang girls and gang boys: Results from a multi-site survey. *Youth and Society* 31: 27–53.

Esbensen, F., B. Brick, C. Melde, K. Tusinski, and T. Taylor. 2008. The role of race and ethnicity in gang membership. In van Gemert, F., Paterson, D., and Lien, I. (eds.), *Youth gangs, migration, and ethnicity.* Uffculme, Devon, UK: Willan Publishing Co.

Esbensen, F., D. Peterson, T. Taylor, and A. Freng. 2010. *Youth violence: Sex and race differences in offending, victimization, and gang membership.* Philadelphia: Temple University Press.

Etter, G. 2001. Totemism and symbolism in white supremacist movements: Images of an urban tribal warrior culture. *Journal of Gang Research* 8: 49–75.

Etter, G. and W. Swymeler. 2008. Examining the demographics of street gangs in Wichita, KS. *Journal of Gang Research* 16: 1.

Federal Bureau of Investigation. 2010. *Crime in the United States, 2009.* Washington, D.C.: FBI.

Finlay, T. and C. Matthews. 1996. *Motorcycle gangs: A literature search.* Toronto, Canada: University of Toronto.

Fleisher, M. 1998. *Dead end kids: Gang girls and the boys they know.* Madison, WI: University of Wisconsin Press.

Fleisher, M. 2006. *Societal and correctional context of prison gangs.* Cleveland: Case Western Reserve University, Mandel School of Applied Social Sciences.

Fleisher, M. and S. Decker. 2001. An overview of the challenge of prison gangs. *Corrections Management Quarterly* 5: 1–9.

Fleisher, M. and J. Krienert. 2004. Life course events, social networks, and the emergence of violence among female gang members. *Journal of Community Psychology* 32: 607–622.

Florida Department of Corrections. 2009. *Major Prison Gangs.* Available at http://www.dc.state.fj.us/pub/gangs/prison.html (Retrieved August 24, 2011).

Fortune, S. 2003. *Inmate and prison gang leadership.* (Unpublished) PhD diss., East Tennessee State University.

Fox, J. and M. Zawitz. 2005. *Homicide trends in the United States.* Washington, D.C.: Bureau of Justice Statistics.

Friedman, W., A. Lurigio, and R. Greenleaf. 2004. Encounters between police officers and youths: The social costs of disrespect. *Journal of Crime and Justice* 27: 1–25.

Gaes, G., S. Wallace, and E. Gilman. 2002. The influence of prison gang affiliation on violence and other prison misconduct. *Prison Journal* 825: 359–383.

Genelin, M. 1993. Gang prosecution. In A. Goldstein and C. Huff (eds.), *The gang intervention handbook*. Champaign, IL: Research Press.

Goldstein, A. 1993. Gang intervention: A historical review. In A. Goldstein and C. Huff (eds.), *The gang intervention handbook*. Champaign, IL: Research Press.

Goldstein, A. and B. Glick. 1994. *The prosocial gang: Implementing aggression replacement training*. Thousand Oaks, CA: Sage.

Gorowitz Institute. 2002. *Dangerous convictions: An introduction to extremist activities in prisons*. New York: Antidefamation League.

Gottfredson, G. and D. Gottfredson. 2001. *Gang problems and gang programs in a national sample of schools*. Washington, D.C.: Government Printing Office.

Guagliardo, J. and M. Langston. 1997. Introducing gang evidence against a criminal defendant at trial: A view from the perspective of the prosecutor and the gang expert witness. *Journal of Gang Research* 4: 1–10.

Hagedorn, J. and M. Devitt. 1991. Fighting female. The social construction of female gangs. In M. Chesney-Lind and Hagedorn J. (eds.), *Female gangs in America: Essays on girls, gangs, and gender* (pp. 256–276). Chicago: Lake View.

Hall, N. 2005. Behind the patch: Angels ABC's. *The Vancouver Sun*, June 10, p. 1.

Harrell, E. 2005. *Violence by gang members. 1993–2003*. Washington, D.C.: Bureau of Justice Statistics.

Hawkins, J., R. Catalano, and J. Miller. 1992. Risk and protective factors for alcohol and other drug problems in adolescence and early adulthood: Implications for substance abuse prevention. *Psychological Bulletin*, 112: 64–105.

Hells Angels Motorcycle Club. 2002. *Drugs and crime*. Washington, D.C.: National Drug Intelligence Center.

Hirschi, T. 1969. *Causes of delinquency*. Berkeley, CA: University of California Berkeley Press.

Howell, J. 1999. Youth gang homicides: A literature review. *Crime and Delinquency* 45: 208–241.

Howell, J. 2003. *Preventing and reducing juvenile delinquency: April comprehensive framework*. Thousand Oaks, CA: Sage Publications.

Howell, J. and J. Lynch. 2000. *Youth gangs in school*. Washington, D.C.: Government Printing Office.

Huff, R. 1998. Comparing the criminal behavior of youth gangs and at-risk youths. *National Institute of Justice Research in Brief* 1–14.

Hutson, H. and M. Eckstein. 1996. Drive-by shootings by violent street gangs in Los Angeles: A five-year review from 1989 to 1993. *Academic Emergency Medicine* 3: 300–303.

Hutson, H., D. Anglin, W. Mallon, and M. Pratt. 1994. Caught in the crossfire of gang violence: Small children as innocent victims of drive-by shootings. *Journal of Emergency Medicine* 12: 385–388.

Hutson, H., D. Anglin, and M. Pratt. 1994. Adolescents and children injured or killed in drive-by shootings in Los Angeles. *New England Journal of Medicine* 330: 324–327.

Hutson, H., D. Anglin, D. Kyriacou, J. Hart, and K. Spears. 1995. The epidemic of gang-related homicides in Los Angeles from 1979–1994. *JAMA: Journal of the American Medical Association* 274: 1031–1036.

Jackson, M. and E. Sharpe. 1997. Prison gang research: Preliminary findings in Eastern North Carolina. *Journal of Gang Research* 5: 1–7.

Jeremiah, D. 2008. Angels: The strange and mysterious truth. New York: Multnomah Publishers.

Joe, K. and M. Chesney-Lind. 1995. Just another mother's angel: An analysis of gender and ethnic variations in youth membership. *Gender and Society* 9: 408–431.

Johnson, W. 1981. Motorcycle gangs and white collar crime. http://www.ncjrs/app/publications/abstract.aspx?ID=147211 (Retrieved February 12, 2011).

Jones, B. 2001. *Bike lust*. Madison, WI: University of Wisconsin Press.

Joseph, J. 2008. Gangs and gang violence in school. *Journal of Gang Research* 16: 44–50.

Katz, C. and V. Webb. 2004. *Police response to gangs: April multisite study*. Phoenix: Arizona State University West, Department of Criminal Justice and Criminology.

Katz, C. and V. Webb. 2006. *Policing gangs in America*. New York: Cambridge University Press.

Klein, M. 1971. *Street gangs and street workers*. Englewood Cliffs, NJ: Prentice Hall.

Klein, M. 1995. *The American street gang*. New York: Oxford University Press.

Klein, M. and C. Maxson. 1989. Street gang violence. In M. Wolfgang and N. S. Weiner (eds.), *Violent crime, violent criminals* (pp. 198–234). Newbury Park, CA: Sage.

Klein, M., C. Maxson, and L. Cunningham. 1991. Crack, street gangs, and violence. *Criminology* 29: 623–650.

Knox, G. 2000. A national assessment of gangs and security threat groups (STGs) in adult correctional institutions: Results of the 1999 Adult Correctional Survey. *Journal of Gang Research* 7: 2–45.

Knox, G. 2005. *The problems of gangs and security threat groups (STGs) in American prisons today: Recent research findings from the 2004 prison gang survey*. Peotone, Il: National Gang Crime Research Center.

Knox, G. 2006. Findings from Kevorkian-12 survey project: April special report of the NGCRC on gang problems in schools. *Journal of Gang Research* 14: 1–52.

Kobring, S., J. Puntil and E. Peluso. 1968. Criteria of status among street groups. In J.F. Short, Jr. (Ed.), *Gang Delinquency and Delinquent Subcultures* (pp. 177–198). New York: J & J. Harper.

Kubrin, C. and T. Wadsworth. 2003. Identifying the structural correlates of African-American killings. *Homicide Studies* 7: 3–35.

Kuhns, J., R. Maguire, and S. Cox. 2007. Public safety concerns among law enforcement agencies in suburban and rural America. *Police Quarterly* 10: 429–454.

Kyriacou, D., H. Hutson, D. Anglin, C. Peek, and J. Kraus. 1999. The relationship between socioeconomic factors and gang violence in the city of Los Angeles. *The Journal of Trauma, Injury, Infection, and Critical Care* 46 (2): 334–339.

Langton, J. 2010. *Showdown: How the Outlaws, Hells Angels, and cops fought for control of the streets*. New York: John Wiley & Sons.

Lattimore, P., R. Linster, and J. MacDonald. 1997. Risk of death among serious young offenders. *Journal of Research in Crime and Delinquency* 34: 187–209.

Laub, J. and J. Lauritsen. 1998. The interdependence of school violence with neighborhood and family conditions. In D. S. Elliot, B. Hamburg, and K. Williams (eds.), *Violence in American schools* (pp. 127–155). Cambridge, U.K.: Cambridge University Press.

Lauderback, D., J. Hansen, and D. Waldorf. 1992. Sisters are doin' it for themselves: A black female gangs in San Francisco. *Gang Journal* 1: 57–72.

Lavigne, Y. 1996. *Hell's Angels: Into the abyss.* New York: Harper Collins.

Lemmer, T., G. Bensinger, and A. Lurigio. 2008. An analysis of police responses to gangs in Chicago. *Police Practice and Research* 9: 417–430.

Lindsey, T. 2005. *A brief history of Outlaw Motorcycle Clubs.* New York: International Journal of Motorcycle Clubs. http://ijms.nova.edu/November2005/IJMS_Artcl. Dulaney.html (Retrieved August 10, 2011).

Lopez, D. 2006. Asian gang homicides and weapons: *Journal of Gang Research* 13: 15–29.

Mallory, S. 2007. *Understanding organized crime.* Boca Raton, FL: Jones and Bartlett.

Marzulli, J. 2009. Pagans biker gang plotted to kill Hell's Angels with grenade attacks, says Feds. *New York Daily News*, October.

Maxson, C. 1999. Gang homicide. In M. Smith and M. Zahn (eds.), *Studying and preventing homicide* (pp. 197–220). Thousand Oaks, CA: Sage.

Maxson, C. and M. Whitlock. 2002. Joining the gang: Gender differences in risk factors for gang membership. In C. R. Huff (ed.) *Gangs in America* (3rd ed.) (pp. 19–36). Thousand Oaks, CA: Sage Publications.

Maxson, C., M. Gordon, and M. Klein. 1985. Differences between gang and nongang homicides. *Criminology* 23 :209–222.

McCorkle, R. and T. Meithe. 2001. *Panic: Rhetoric and reality in the war on street gangs.* Upper Saddle River, NJ: Prentice Hall.

McEnry, C. 2010. Personal interview. San Francisco, December 14.

McGloin, J. 2007. The organizational structure of street gangs in Newark, NJ. A network analysis methodology. *Journal of Gang Research* 15: 1–34.

Miller, J. 1998. Gender and victimization risk among young women in gangs. *Journal of Research in Crime and Delinquency* 35: 429–453.

Miller, J. 2001a. Young women's involvement in gangs in the United States: An overview. In M. Kelin, H. Kerner, and E. Weitekamp, E. (eds.), *The Eurogang paradox: Street gangs and youth gangs in the U.S. and Europe.* Boston and Dordrecht, The Netherlands: Kluwer Academic.

Miller, J. 2001b. One of the guys: Girls, gangs, and gender. New York: Oxford University Press.

Miller, J. 2002. The girls in the gang: What we've learned from two decades of research. In C. Ronald Huff (ed.), *Gangs in America* (pp. 175–197). Thousand Oaks, CA: Sage.

Miller, J. and R. Brunson. 2000. Gender dynamics in youth gangs: A comparison of male and female accounts. *Justice Quarterly* 17: 801–830.

Miller, J. and S. Decker. 2001. Young women and gang violence: Gender, street offending, and violent victimization in gangs. *Justice Quarterly* 18: 115–140.

Miller, P. 2010. Personal interview. Department of Justice. Baltimore, MD.

Miller, W. 1966. Violent crimes in city gangs. *Annals of the American Academy of Political and Social Sciences.* 364: 96–112.

Moore, J. 1991. *Going down the barrio.* Philadelphia: Temple University Press.

Moore, J. 1994. The chola life course: Chicana heroin users and the barrio gang. *International Journal of Addiction* 29: 1115–1126.

Moore, J. 1998. Understanding youth street gangs: Economic restructuring and the urban underclass. In M. Watts (ed.), *Cross-cultural perspectives on youth and violence* (pp. 65–78). Stamford, CT. JAI Press.

Moore, J. and T. Hagedorn. 1996. What happens to girls in the gang? In C. Ronald Huff (ed.), *Gangs in America* (pp. 205–218). Thousand Oaks, CA: Sage.

National Center for Women and Policing. 2002. *Equality denied: The status of women in policing: 2001*. Beverly Hills, CA: National Center for Women and Policing.

National Drug Intelligence Center. 2002. No. 2002-M0148-002. Washington, D.C.

National Gang Intelligence Center. 2009. *National gang threat assessment*. Crystal City, VA: U.S. Department of Justice.

National Youth Gang Center. 2000. *1998 national youth gang survey*. Washington, D.C.: U.S. Department of Justice.

Newbold, G. and G. Dennehy. 2003. Girls in gangs: Biographies and culture of female gang associates in New Zealand. *Journal of Gang Research*. 11: 33–53.

Nurge, D. 2008. Gang females. In L. Kontos and D. Brotherton (eds.), *Encyclopedia of gangs* (pp. 61–64). Westport, CT: Greenwood Press.

O'Dell, B. 2010. Informant at Virginia biker trial talks of gang "war." The SunNews. com. October 26. (Retrieved December 7, 2010.)

Oliver, R. 2002. Incident in Nevada first multiple slaying in casino. *Las Vegas Review-Journal*, April 28.

Papachristos, A. 2009. Murder by structure: Dominance relations and the social structure of gang homicide. *American Journal of Sociology* 115: 74–128.

Parascandola, R., J. Martinez, and H. Kennedy. 2010. Police look for link between C4 Explosives in Manhattan cemetery and bizarre note found nearby. *New York Daily News*, November 10, p. 1.

Pazzano, S. 2010. Snitch was Hell's Angels enforcer. http://cnews.canoe, a/CNEWS/Crime/2010/11/161177606.html (Retrieved July 29, 2011).

Peirce, P. 2009. Inner workings of the Pagans motorcycle gang slowly being revealed. *The Pittsburg Tribune Review News Service*, July 4.

Peterson, D., J. Miller, and F. Esbensen. 2001. The impact of sex composition on gangs and gang member delinquency. *Criminology* 39: 411–439.

Pizarro, J. and J. McGloin. 2006. Explaining gang homicides in Newark, NJ: Collective behavior or social disorganization. *Journal of Criminal Justice* 34: 195–207.

Pizarro, J., N. Corsaro, and S. Yu. 2007. Journey to crime and victimization: An application of routine activities theory and environmental criminology to homicide. *Victims and Offenders* 2: 375–394.

Pratt, A. 2006. *Motorcycle nihilism, and the price of cool*. Chicago: Open Court Publishing.

Pugmire, L. and A. Covarrubias. 2006. *22 motorcycle club members arrested in raids in 5 counties*. http://articles.latimes.com/mar/10/local/me-vargos10 (Retrieved Aug. 24, 2011).

Rand, A. 1987. Transitional life events and desistance from delinquency and crime. In M. Wolfgang, T. Thornberry, and R. Figlio (eds.), *From boy to man, from delinquency to crime* (pp. 134–162). Chicago: University of Chicago Press.

Richardson, A. 1991. U.S.A. perspective on outlaw motorcycle gangs. Paper presented at the 17th annual Motorcycle Gang Conference. September. Orlando, FL.

Rijn, N., P. Edwards, and R. Brennan. 2006. Biker gangs linked to murders. *The Toronto Star*. Toronto, Ontario, April 10, A1.

Rivers, D. 2010. Personal interview. Orlando, FL, December 6.

Roberts, A. 2007. Predictors of homicide clearance by arrest: An event history analysis of NIBRS incidents. *Homicide Studies* 11: 82–93.

Robinson, P., W. Boscardin, S. George, S. Teklehaimanot, K. Henslin, and R. Bluthenthal. 2009. The effects of urban street gangs densities on small area homicide incidences in a large metropolitan county, 1994–2002. *Journal of Urban Health* 86: 511–523.

Ross, J. 2008. Gangs in prison. In L. Kontos and D. Brotherton (eds.), *Encyclopedia of gangs* (pp. 98–102). Westport, CT: Greenwood Press.

Sanders, R. 2010. Personal interview. Louisville, KY, December 10.

Sanders, W. 1994. *Gangbangs and drive-bys: Grounded culture and juvenile gang violence.* New York: Aldine.

Schmalleger, F. and J. Smykla. 2007. *Corrections in the 21st century,* 3rd ed. New York: McGraw-Hill.

Serwer, A. 1992. The Hell's Angels devilish business. *Fortune Magazine,* November 30, pp. 63–66.

Shelden, R. 2005. Gangs. In M. Bosworth (ed.), *Encyclopedia of prisons and correctional facilities* (pp. 359–362), Vol. 1. Thousand Oaks, CA: Sage.

Shelden, R., Tracy, S. and Brown, W. 2004. *Youth gangs in American society.* Belmont, CA: Wadsworth Press.

Short, J. 1989. Exploring integration of theoretical levels of explanation. Notes on gang delinquency. In S. Krohn, M. Krohn, and A. Liska (eds.), *Theoretical integration in the study of deviance and crime: problems and prospects.* Albany, NY: State University of New York Press.

Short, J. and I. Nye. 1958. Reported behavior as a criterion of deviant behavior. *Social Problems* 5: 207–213.

Spergel, I. 1990. Youth gangs: continuity and change. In M. Tonry, and N. Morris (eds.), *Crime and justice: April review of research* (Vol. 12). Chicago: University of Chicago Press.

Spergel, I. 1995. *The youth gang problem: A community approach.* New York: Oxford University Press.

Spergel, I. and G. Curry. 1990. Strategies and perceived agency effectiveness in dealing with the youth gang problem. In C. Huff (ed.), *Gangs in America.* Thousand Oaks, CA: Sage Publishers.

Thornberry, T. 1998. Membership in youth gangs and involvement in serious and violent offending. In R. Loerber and F. Farrington (eds.), *Serious and violent juvenile offenders: Risk factors and successful interventions* (pp. 147–166). Thousand Oaks, CA: Sage.

Thompkins, D. 2000. School violence: Gangs and a culture of fear. *The ANNALS of the American Academy of Political and Social Science* 567: 54–71.

Thompson, H. 1965. The motorcycle gangs. *The Nation* May 17: 1–8.

Thompson, H. 1996. *Hell's Angels: A strange and terrible saga.* New York: Random House.

Thompson, H. 1999. *Hell's Angels: A strange and terrible saga.* New York: Modern Library.

Thompson, T. 2009. *Hell's Angels: A strange and terrible saga.* New York: Modern Library.

Thornberry, T. and M. Krohn. 2003. *Taking stock of delinquency: An overview of findings from contemporary longitudinal studies.* New York: Kluwer/Plenum Publishers.

Tita, G. and J. Cohen. 2004. Measuring spatial diffusion of shots fired activity across city neighborhoods. In M. F. Goodchild and D. G. Janelle (eds.), *Spatially integrated social science* (pp. 171–204). New York: Oxford Press.

Tita, G. and G. Ridgeway. 2007. The impact of gang formation on local patterns of crime. *Journal of Research in Crime and Delinquency* 44: 208–237.

Tita, G., J. Cohen, and J. Engberg. 2005. An ecological study of the location of gang "set space." *Social Problems* 52: 272–299.

Trethewy, S. and T. Katz. 1998. *Motorcycle gangs or motorcycle mafia.* http://www.ncjrs.gov/app/publications (Retrieved August 24, 2011).

United States Bureau of the Census. 2009. *American Community Survey, 2009.* Washington, D.C.

Vago, S. 1994. *Law and society,* 4th ed. Englewood Cliffs, NJ: Prentice Hall.

Valentine, B. 2000. *Gangs and their tattoos: Identifying gangbangers on the street and in prison.* Boulder, CO: Paladin Press.

Van Derbeken, J. 2008. Hell's Angels leader in S.F. shot dead in fight. *The San Francisco Chronicle,* September 3, B-1.

Vogel, E. 2005. Laughlin riot: Court hears biker case. *Las Vegas Review-Journal,* November 18.

Weisel, D.L., and E. Painter. 1997. *The Police Response to Gangs: Case Studies of Five Cities.* Washington, DC: Police Executive Research Forum.

Weisel, D. and T. Shelley. 2004. *Specialized gang units: Form and functions in community policing.* Washington, D.C.: U.S. Department of Justice.

Wethren, G. and V. Colnett. 2008. *A wayward angel: The full story of the Hell's Angels.* New York: The Lyons Press.

Winterhalder, E. 2005. *Out in bad standing: Inside the Bandidos Motorcycle Club: The making of a worldwide dynasty.* Owasso, OK: Blockhead City Press.

Winterhalder, E. 2008. *The assimilation: Rock machine become Bandidos—Bikers united against the Hell's Angels.* London: ECW Press.

Wood, J.L. and J.R. Adler. 2001. Gang activity in English prisons: The staff perspective. Psychology, Crime and Law, 7: 167–192.

Wyrick, P. and J. Howell. 2004. Strategic risk-based response to youth gangs. *Juvenile Justice* 9: 20–29.

Yablonski, L. 1962. *The violent gang.* New York: Macmillan.

Internet Resources

http://homepage.tinet.ie/~rockedge/hri/history.htm (Retrieved August 24, 2011).

http://www.gangsorus.com (accessed August 24, 2011).

http://www.hells-angels/?=charters.

http://www.woai.com/most popular/story.asp?/content-id-d30dce-483a-9424-fb66-fi3a6260 (Retrieved June 12, 2011).

Index